SONS OF THE SEAS

SONS OF THE SEAS

Patrick Gaffney

Matador
9 Priory Business Park,
Wistow Road, Kibworth Beauchamp,
Leicestershire. LE8 0RX
Tel: 0116 279 2299
Email: books@troubador.co.uk
Web: www.troubador.co.uk/matador
Twitter: @matadorbooks

ISBN 978 1784624 347

British Library Cataloguing in Publication Data.
A catalogue record for this book is available from the British Library.

Printed and bound in the UK by TJ International, Padstow, Cornwall
Typeset in 11pt Aldine by Troubador Publishing Ltd, Leicester, UK

Matador is an imprint of Troubador Publishing Ltd

Dedicated to all sailors who have sailed the seas in the service of their country in both war and peace.

ONE

WIND AND SAILS

My father, Harry Cecil Gaffney, was born with the sea in his blood, and salt in his veins. He was a master mariner of the old school, and through experience, skill, and generous doses of good fortune, he was a survivor.

Born on the 11th November 1893 in Wharfedale, Yorkshire he was sent to Framlington College in Suffolk where the family had moved to. At sixteen years of age he was sent to the training ship, H.M.S. *Conway* to be trained as a young cadet for a life at sea. The *Conway*, at the time being moored in the River Mersey off Rock Ferry, Liverpool.

Lads from the *Conway* going ashore.

H.M.S. *Conway* began her life as H.M.S. *Nile* in 1839. She was designed by Sir Robert Seppings, a famous naval architect. In 1875 the *Nile* was allocated on loan to the Mercantile Marine Service Association as a training ship and after being fitted out for her duties, she was renamed H.M.S. *Conway*.

The ship remained in the Mersey until the Second World War when a decision was made to move her to safer waters in the Menai Straits, near Bangor, where another training ship had once been moored. In 1949 H.M.S. *Conway* was towed under the two bridges crossing the Menai Straits to moorings near Plas Newydd, Anglesey where she would continue to train cadets for sea. In 1953 H.M.S. *Conway* was due to be refitted in Birkenhead and preparations were made to tow the ship under the two bridges once more. However, disaster struck, and the ship was grounded between the two bridges. H.M.S. *Conway* subsequently caught fire and burned to the water line.

Whilst at H.M.S. *Conway* Harry's parents paid £22.15 a term in fees. He was made a junior cadet captain, and coxswain of the dinghy, which was used to ferry the cadets ashore. His application, and character, was assessed as Very Good.

After my father left the *Conway* in February 1911 he was drafted to the three-masted barque *Inversnaid* to serve a three-year apprentice at sea.

The *Inversnaid* was a steel hull barque built in Dumbarton in 1892 and was built for the Inver Line and owned by George Milne and Co. She weighed in at 1414 tons, a length of 238 feet, and a draught of 21 feet. Once on board the *Inversnaid*, they sailed on the long passage to the South American continent for the port of Buenos Aires. No doubt the *Inversnaid* spent many a long day at sea in all types of weather, particularly rounding the Cape Horn.

In his book *The Last of the Windjammers* Vol.11, Basil Lubbock gives a brief history of the *Inversnaid*. She survived World War I and shortly afterwards she was sold along with two other 'Inver' barques to Sir William Garthwaite, a shipping insurer from Montreal. In 1922 he re-named her the *Garthsnaid* and continued plying her trade on the South American continent. Not long after the *Garthsnaid* outward bound from Iquique (Chile) to Melbourne, Australia found herself in a severe storm off Gabo Island just south of the port of Melbourne. The White Star liner *Zealandic* outward bound from Sydney found the *Garthsnaid* lying in a helpless condition with the main mast gone, her foretop mast hanging over the side, her mizzen top mast missing, her decks a tangle of twisted and broken rigging, and all her boats staved in.

Captain Jones of the *Zealandic* at once decided to tow the lame duck into port, but the weather was bad, and it was only after four unsuccessful attempts that a steel hawser was at last got aboard the *Garthsnaid*. Her crew had been without sleep and with scarcely any food for three days, and were so weak that it took them three hours to heave in the hawser by the capstan and make it fast around the base of the mast. Eventually she was towed from Gabo Island into Melbourne after a long and difficult struggle. The author does not mention what happened next but we can only assume she never sailed again.

During his three-year voyage on the *Inversnaid* Harry had passed the exams for Boson Mate 3rd. Class, and Boson Mate 2nd.Class. He had learnt Spanish, as all the officers and cadets on board were expected to do, to enable them to converse with the local traders.

On his return to England Harry found that war had been declared and was called up for service in the Royal Navy, and enrolled as a midshipman.

On Saturday 15th August Harry left Southampton on a troop ship bound for Simons Town to join H.M.S. *Kinsfaun Castle*.

TWO

THE CAPE STATION

The *Kinsfauns Castle* was built in 1899 for the Union Castle Line. She was a steel twin screw steamer of 9664 tons. She could accommodate 266 first-class, 171 second-class, and 198 third-class passengers. She was used as a mail ship, and her run was from London to Cape Town. At the outbreak of WWI the Admiralty requisitioned many merchant ships to see service in the Royal Navy. The *Kinsfaun Castle* was one of these ships and was converted from a passenger ship to an armed merchant cruiser and troop ship.

From 1914 to 1918 the *Kinsfaun Castle* was used for troop-carrying duties mainly in the Mediterranean and to Mesopotarnia. In 1919 she was returned to her owners where she continued her duties as a passenger and mail carrier on the Cape Town run. She left Cape Town for the last time in November 1926 and then was briefly chartered from January to April 1927 to carry troops from Southampton to Shanghai. A few months later she was sold to Dutch breakers and broken up for scrap in Rotterdam.

However, on Saturday15[th] August 1914 in squally weather, my father, as a young probationary midshipman, boarded H.M.S. *Kinsfaun Castle* at Southampton Docks bound for the Cameroons in German West Africa. She was to land troops in the action now taking place at Duala.

After two days at sea, during the dog watches he noted in his log book that the ship was at Latitude 44.53 North and Longitude 8.11 West. He also noted the crew had changed into wearing ducks as the temperatures were increasing although they were not yet in the tropics.

The gun crews drilled daily, and they would stop all ships that they came across. In the event the ship in question did not stop, a blank round would be fired.

The following day they received a wireless message that the *Kaiser Wilhelm der Grosse* (20,000 tons; speed 22 knots) had captured the Union Castle SS *Gallicia* and was possibly in the vicinity. The captain ordered the funnels painted in Union Castle colours so if she sighted us she would think we were on a mail run. We would then turn tail, but as she was much faster than us she would overtake us. At that point we would then turn round and fire on her.

Many of the British ships they intercepted did not even know that war had been declared.

On Saturday 22nd August 1914, in the early hours of the morning (00:30), we came across a four-masted barque which, after displaying the searchlight on her, proved to be the German barque *Werner Vinnen* of Brennen (3145 tons) bound from Cardiff to Caleta Coloso on the west coast of South America, with a full consignment of coal. She was given orders to shorten sail, and training our guns on her, we stood by until daylight. At this time we sent a boarding officer to declare her a Prize of War. The white ensign was then hoisted, with the German flag below it.

The captain decided to send her to Sierra Leone, so sent a prize crew aboard which consisted of thirty-two all told. Needless to say they were all well armed. All firearms and valuables of the German crew were confiscated. The crew of the prize consisted of thirty-four men, one of which was an Englishman, one a Russian, one a Swede, and the remainder Germans. They were all willing to work the ship to port on condition that the captain gave them their parole, which he did. However, later three refused to work the ship, preferring to come on board as prisoners of war, which more or less amounts to being passengers. This was their first initiation of war, as they had left Cardiff on the 1st August. Still they took it very well and seemed quite delighted because their hides will be safe now at any rate. The captain was a bit upset because he had some money in the ship, and more so because he was naturally very fed up with the German policy.

We parted company with her at 9am and directed our

course to St.Vincent where after a twenty-four-hour stay we received orders to proceed to Cape Town, via St. Helena. Whilst at sea they received the news that H.M.S. *Highflyer* had sunk the German ship *Kaiser Wilhelm Der Grosse*.

Crossing the International Dateline King Neptune came aboard and christened some forty odd men. Aside from this jolly time, a man was arrested on board for pulling a knife on a shipmate.

Further orders received meant that the ship would now miss St. Helena and sail direct to Simons Town. At this time there were many ships carrying troops belonging to the South African Mounted Rifles up from Cape Town to parts of the western coastline.

On Friday 11th November 1914, the *Kinsfaun Castle* arrived in Simons Town which at that time was under martial law with thousands of troops keeping order. The Liverpool collier *Drumlanrig* came alongside and the rest of the week was spent coaling ship. Besides coaling they also loaded on board eighty lyddite shells for bombarding purposes. She also took on board a Curtiss hydroplane which had been given to the Navy by a private citizen.

The K.C. was now made the flagship of the Cape station with Rear Admiral King-Hall in command.

On Sat. 19th November the K.C. sailed from Simons Town bound for Walfish Bay which they expected to arrive at on the following Monday. The wind was blowing hard and there was a big swell. Due to the shallow water at Walfish Bay the ship had to anchor two miles off shore arriving at 2pm.

After coaling, the ship steamed to the east coast of Africa where a Royal Naval squadron consisting of the light cruiser H.M.S. *Challenger*, the monitor H.M.S. *Severn* and several other ships were blockading the German light cruiser *Konigsberg*. The German cruiser was anchored up the Rufiji River Delta approximately a 100 miles south of Dar es Salaam.

The Rufiji River runs into the Indian Ocean about a 100 miles south of Zanzibar. The river fans out into smaller tributaries as it nears the coast making four different entrances into the river from seaward. The river is 370 miles long and is formed by the confluence of the Kilombero and Luwegu Rivers which were infested with crocodiles and water snakes. Amongst other wildlife were the giant green turtles, some weighing as much as 400 lbs. Along it's banks were the largest mango forests in East Africa.

Up this river lay the most powerful ship in the German Navy stationed in the Indian Ocean.

The *Konigsberg* had been built at Kaiserliche Werft in Kiel and was launched on December 12th 1905. She had a crew of fourteen officers, and just over 300 ratings. She was 378 feet in length with 3-inch armour plating down both sides, but with her twin triple expansion engines could still reach a speed of 24 knots. She was heavily armed with ten 4.1-inch guns. Two mountings side by side up front, three each side, down the length of the ship, and two more mountings on the back end. Ten further 3-inch guns were also strategically placed around the ship. In addition she carried two 18-inch torpedoes. Before joining the High Seas Fleet, SMS *Konigsberg* was used as an escort ship for Kaiser Wilhelm II's yacht.

November 1908 in company with the new armoured cruiser *Scharnhorst*, and the dispatch boat *Sleipner*, she escorted Wilhelm II's yacht on a visit to Portsmouth and a trip up the Thames. Whilst there, the ship was visited by Queen Wilhelmina of the Netherlands.

She then went on training cruises in the North Sea, Atlantic, and the Baltic. On the 1st April 1914 Fregattenkapitan (Corvette Captain) Max Looff took command and left Wilhelmshaven for a two-year commission on the German East African station.

Whilst on station, in August 1914 war between Germany and Britain was declared. The *Konigsberg* received orders to sink British shipping around the entrance to the Red Sea. A lack of coal hampered Looff's efforts as the British prevented his collier from leaving Dar es Salaam and purchased all the coal in Portuguese East Africa to deny it to the *Konigsberg*.

However, the *Konigsberg* came across a British freighter, the *City of Winchester*, off the coast of Oman. A prize crew took the ship and the 1200 tons of coal she was carrying.

The following month, she completely surprised the British cruiser H.M.S. *Pegasus* and after a fierce fight, the *Pegasus* was sent to the bottom.

The *Konigsberg* now sought refuge in the Rufiji River because of engine failure, and was awaiting spare parts to come over land from Dar Es Salaam. She had tried to disguise her presence there by spreading trees and all kinds of vegetation around the ship to make the ship meld into the surrounding countryside. The Navy had made several attempts before to go after her, but all had been unsuccessful. The *Kingsfaun Castle* could not get up the river because of the many sandbanks and its shallow depth. It had never been surveyed and no charts existed.

However on the 12th November 1914 H.M.S. *Chatham*, having taken all the coal out of the collier *Newbridge* of London, with an armed party on board, started to steam up the river followed by two picket boats. When three miles up, they were suddenly attacked from the banks of the river by a party of marines from the *Konigsberg*, which was hiding in the thick mango forest. The *Chatham* boarding party returned fire and a fierce exchange of small arms fire ensued. As a result of this action three crew members were killed and a further fifteen were wounded.

Proceeding another mile upriver she came across the SS *Somalia* which was full of coal to supply the *Konigsberg*. *Chatham* opened fire and sent her and the cargo to the bottom. The *Chatham* then sunk the two colliers that had accompanied her. This was all part of the plan to block this part of the river which was quite narrow, then turned back down the river towards the sea entrance. She would proceed to Zanzibar to bury her dead and land her wounded but was expected to return to the squadron the following day.

The *Konigsberg*, even if it had been fully functional, faced a very uncertain future, with very few options. She would have to come out fighting. Attempting to leave the mouth of the river she would be met by several light cruisers of the British fleet who were stationed directly outside the exits.

The *Kinsfaun Castle* now sailed up the east coast to Zanibar to find the elusive German light cruiser *Konigsberg* which was protecting the German colonies in that part of Africa for the last three years.

The Admiralty had now decided to have two flat-bottomed monitors, H.M.S. *Severn* and H.M.S. *Mersey*, to be towed from Malta, to resolve the situation. They were for all intents and purposes floating gun platforms that packed a considerable punch. They had a draught of only five feet, but carried two 6-inch guns, two 4.7 mountings, and four 3-pounders. An additional three-pounder was carried strictly for protection against aircraft.

In late November the K.C. was off Niororo Island and early in the morning at 5:30 had launched her seaplane to find the exact location of the *Konigsberg*. She flew at 3000 feet but the weather was quite unfavourable, the sky being very cloudy. It was getting quite late in the day, and as the plane had failed to return the K.C. weighed anchor in search of it. Soon after getting to sea she saw a dhow flying the German flag. Coming alongside her they took off the crew and the cargo then sunk her. At 1:30 that afternoon they sighted the plane off Okuza Island. My father further records in his records: we sent two boats.

One, to bring the plane back, and the other, the aviator, whom we spotted in the water. On his arrival we gave him a hearty welcome. It appeared that after he left he got up to about 3000 feet and got lost in the clouds, and after flying for two hours, he planed down, got the machine ashore, or rather up on the beach, went ashore himself and tried to light a fire with his revolver. On his return the tide had come up so swiftly that his plane had got adrift, so he had just started to swim out to her when we came on the scene. He is none the worse for his adventure and will probably have another go tomorrow.

The plane was hoisted inboard, and the K.C. now sailed towards the mouth of the Rufiji River. On arrival, two days later, the plane was launched again and returned after a very successful flight. The pilot had found the exact position of the *Konigsberg*, saw that she was freshly painted, anchored facing seaward, she being in a different creek altogether to the one we thought she was in.

Monday 23rd November the K.C. received orders to go to Durban. On arriving there she set about coaling ship. Once she had coaled she left harbour. The seaplane had been stripped and put back together and was once again fit for flying. Guns crews were drilled daily, and the midshipman received bayonet practice.

Information received from spies re: *Konigsberg*.

1. She had got three holes in her above the water line which had been boarded up. This being as a result of H.M.S. *Chatham*'s firing at her from 14,000 yards.
2. It is highly likely she has a considerable casualty list.
3. That she is short of coal, she having to be taken upriver by means of wood fuel.
4. They are also cut off from all communication with the numerous islands which they have been obtaining cattle from.
5. They have employed about 200 natives at four pence per day to dig trenches.

In early December the K.C. was at the mouth of the Rufiji River. The *Konigsberg* can only escape from one-and-a-half hours before to one-and-a-half hours after high water, so the anxious period consists of about six hours each day. If she fancies her chances and comes out our only chance of damaging her is at the mouth of the river, for once she passes us her superior speed will take her out of danger.

Looking for signs of any movement the ship sent a party of marines ashore. They found an abandoned wireless station, with a lookout tower, with numerous German lager beer bottles. The Marines set the tower and the station alight and burnt it to the ground before returning to the ship.

On Friday 11th Dec. the ship received orders to proceed to Mombasa. This was only a short trip and they arrived the next day. Once alongside they began the arduous task of loading 1500 tons of coal. Coaling went on all day and all night. They eventually finished at 6pm on the Wednesday, and on Friday they left port to sail for Zanzibar arriving on Saturday 19th December.

On passage they intercepted a wireless message being sent out by the *Konigsberg* which gave details of the movements of the K.C. and H.M.S. *Chatham*.

They now steamed to the mouth of the Rufiji River where the whole of the East African Fleet were assembled. The fleet on the station at this time was a considerable force. There were fourteen light cruisers, two patrol boats and four tugs.

Seeing German troops moving ashore, the K.C. opened fire at 4000 yards and scattered them.

Further orders received, the K.C. sailed eighty miles to the south to the German port of Kilwa where at 6000 yards they opened fire on the town. The shore battery returned fire, and a marine on board was killed. However, the shoreside battery was quickly put out of action by the accurate gunnery of the K.C. which pounded it for more than an hour. They then left and went to sea. At 6:30 that evening the engines were stopped and the dead body of the marine was committed to the deep. It was a very impressive scene indeed as he was buried according to service custom, with a firing party, the last post also being sounded.

Christmas Day 1914 at Zanzibar

Received a cable from the King and Queen wishing the ship's company the usual greetings, to which the captain sent a suitable reply.

In the afternoon the crew were allowed ashore and that evening the crew gave a concert which made the day most enjoyable.

Three days later at 4am on Monday the 28th they put to sea and arrived off Dar es Salaam at 8:30am the same day with orders to bombard the town and the trenches around it that were full of German troops. However, heavy rain and thick fog prevented the shoot.

On New Year's Eve H.M.S. *Chatham* sent a wireless message to the *Konigsberg*. "We wish you a happy New Year, hope to see you soon," to which the *Konigsberg* replied, "Thanks: Same to you, we are always at home."

Chatham closed the conversation with, "If you come out we will give you a real British welcome."

In the meantime The K.C. had been to Mombasa

and picked up troops. On Sunday 10th January 1915 after bombarding the shoreline, the troops, with 400 porters and a company of sappers, were landed at Mafia Island. This was achieved without incident. By the following Wednesday the Germans had surrendered unconditionally.

The K.C. proceeded to Bombay to enter dry dock. They would spend the next month there. They took on board two Sopwith biplanes, and after coaling and taking on ammunition, they left, bound once again for Zanzibar. En route a fireman had been killed by an accident in the engine room and was taken ashore for burial once in port.

Seaplane no. 824, whilst alighting on the water after a good flight, hit the water broadside on to the swell and capsized. The pilot and mechanic fortunately escaped injury, which was more than the plane did. Both wings had been smashed and on being examined later, many parts were found to be irreparably damaged. As it would take at least three weeks to fit and repair her, the captains of all the ships had a conference and decided to wire home for another plane. The message was done then and there. The Admiralty wired back that they would send two planes immediately.

Mid-February saw the ship off Niororo Island, a small island of about half a square mile where thirty-six natives lived. They eked out a living by growing Indian corn and a little tropical fruit, combined with fishing and selling mats which they make.

My father went ashore and met the head man. He gave him some tobacco and matches which highly delighted him. He further writes: Also saw an old man writing or rather copying in Arabic from an ancient Koran. He was doing this on a board by means of a piece of wood and a black concoction which acted as a substitute for ink. We learnt that he held the position of school master and was preparing the next day's lesson.

On 1st March 1915, the blockade of the German East Coast began. The British fleet consisted of about ten light cruisers armed with 12- and 3-pounder guns. In addition were two very large tugs. The patrol area for the K.C. was to be south of Mafia Island to the Lindi River.

At 8am the *Kingsfaun Castle* proceeded seven miles up the river to the small island of Kilindoni where they sighted three dhows which they captured. Each dhow had a crew of eight natives who came from Lindi a further three miles upriver. They were taken on board and questioned. We learnt that food supplies to the *Konigsberg* were very scarce, what little there was being practically all commandeered by the Germans, who have 2000 natives working on the plantations for no wages at all. Surely this is slavery. There were no British troops in the immediate area, they having been sent further up country. After taking the three dhows in tow they were handed over to the colonel in charge of the island.

Life on board the ships that ventured up the Rufiji River was never easy. The ships became infested with rats, and cases of smallpox and malaria were not uncommon. When one of the crew members died of malaria, injections were given although supplies were limited. In Harry's case he was injected in the leg, after the first one had no effect at all.

Then, in the middle of March at 4am one morning, the ship received an urgent message from the British India SS *Chakdina*, she having run aground at Niula Reef, Tango. The K.C. proceeded at all possible speed to her assistance. The *Chakdina*, 3080 tons, had been bound from Durban to Bombay, via Zanibar and Mombasa with passengers and mail, with her holds containing 1100 tons of coal. The K.C. reached her at twelve noon and attached a 6-inch towing wire to her, and stood by. The first job was to unload the coal. H.M.S. *Duplex* then arrived with sixty-nine coolies to help in unloading the coal. They worked through the day and night. The following morning the K.C. lowered their lifeboats and began transferring the passengers and mail to the British India ship *Matiana*. By noon 490 tons had been unloaded and with a high tide at 4pm it was decided to make an attempt to refloat her. A six-inch wire was attached, and with the K.C. taking the strain she was refloated.

The ship now left the river delta bound for Mombasa. Orders were for the ship to stay there as there was a severe shortage of coal affecting the whole fleet.

Whilst there, the flagship sent a prisoner on board for us to hand over to the authorities. He was a young guy of about twenty-eight, and spoke English fluently. He was given his meals in the saloon and had a cabin for himself. I took the opportunity to have a conversation with him. He told me he had been on the German East African station for four years, and had been ashore during one of our bombardments. A shell came through the roof of the house where he was staying so he went down the cellar. He said that he was very lucky as the whole house had been demolished. He was also quite firm in his belief that Germany would win the war by August. Harry never did have another chat with him as the next day he was sent to the concentration camp at Nairobi.

It was whilst in Mombasa that the ship got rid of their two seaplanes sending them to the Cunard ship *Laconia* to be taken for repairs.

On Sunday 28th March at 5am the ship left Mombasa and sailed once again for the Rufiji River. Anchoring off Niororo Island the third pin in the shackle of the starboard anchor came out and as a result the anchor and cable ended up on the bottom in a large heap. They buoyed the position and anchored with the port one. The *Weymouth* sent over three divers, and the cable and anchor was heaved inboard and secured up.

At this time the *Goliath* had gone upstream to Lindi. They ordered the magistrate off the island, and gave him a half-hour to send off the 200 Askari soldiers. He did not comply with the demand which of course was only an excuse to bombard the place, which they did when the half was up.

The admiral had strong reasons to believe the *Konigsberg* will attempt to break out of the river at night. The two picket boats patrolling the mouth of the river would fire three rockets as a warning. The *K.C.*, *Weymouth*, and *Hyacinth* would be waiting.

For the next three days the *K.C.* would take on coal, move into a position at the mouth of the river at night. On Monday 12th April the *Pickle* came alongside and the *K.C.* had to give her six-and-a-half tons of coal. This didn't go down very well with the crew, but as the *K.C.*

was the junior ship of the squadron it had no choice but to follow the admiral's orders.

For the rest of the month the *K.C.* patrolled at the mouth of the river Delta. H.M.S. *Laconia* had arrived with the repaired seaplanes and had made four successful flights over the *Konigsberg* at 700 feet, even taking a photograph on one such trip. This was the first time ever that the Navy had taken an aerial picture.

In early May she received orders to proceed to Durban arriving on the 8th May where she immediately began to coal ship. Harry, and Lt. Boothroyd, an ex Cunard Line Officer, left the ship at 8am and motored to his friend who had a farm at Tongaart which is a small village about thirty miles from here. They arrived at 11:30 to a bungalow named 'Graylands' which stood on the crest of a hill. It was quite spacious and well fitted out. On one side it faces the sea, and the Tongaart River. The farm is entirely devoted to fruit growing.

On our arrival we found quite a party going on. The first thing we did was have a bathe in the surf. We were joined in this by a Mrs. Mitcalf and her daughters who also live in the bungalow. We were given a good lunch after which Boothroyd and I returned to the ship. It was possibly the most enjoyable day I have spent since coming on station here.

Thursday 13th May 1915

Harry and his friend Boothroyd had been out fishing, returning on board at 4:30pm. Much to their surprise they found that a landing part of sixty blue jackets, under Lt. Siggers, and four midshipman including myself, had to go ashore immediately to assist the police as serious anti-German riots were taking place.

We soon got ashore and had a special tram to the police station. We were then hustled off to various parts of the town. Previous to going we had instructions to use no violence as the crowd were quite good natured, and everyone was quite in sympathy as you can guess. All we had to do really was to keep them orderly. I had charge of a section of fifteen men and received orders to guard the largest bakery and confectioners in the town.

I arrived at 5:30pm to find all the windows smashed and a large bonfire made up of the carts etc. of the establishment. There was a large crowd outside who gave us quite an ovation on our arrival as it was very apparent to them that we were in full sympathy. They sang 'All the nice girls love a sailor', 'Long way to Tipperary', 'A life on the ocean way', 'Rule Britannia' and the national anthem.

I posted sentries all round the place and paraded up and down myself. Feeling quite important myself in full rig. Females were quite conspicuous amongst the crowd and it was quite impossible to prevent them having a tête-à-tête with the sentries. A very thoughtful lady brought me some tea in a thermos flask.

At 9:00pm we were relieved and went to the police station for some tucker, which we soon finished, as we were called away to the Beach Hotel. I doubled my section up there and arrived with the crowd. We received another ovation there. I formed them up outside the hotel and the crowd demanded the hoisting of the Union Jack, which was done. The manager's wife came out and started to sing the national anthem. My men sprang to attention, whilst I saluted. The good lady, however, only got halfway through then he fainted in my arms.

The crowd dispersed, and then we went to our first place, 'Baumanns', which was now one mass of flames, having been fired after we left. We just managed to keep the crowd back as debris was falling in all directions.

At 12:30 we went back to the police station and, them not requiring our services any longer, we returned to the ship.

There were twenty large fires in the town that day, and the white town was one mass of flames, bonfires being in the streets all over the place. The whole object was to avenge the terrible outrage on the *Lusitania*, which was mentioned many times. No attempt was made to stop the crowd, but we concerned with the safety of the crowd. The crowd were very orderly, and they went about their business in a very systematic manner. Everywhere the intense hatred of the Kaiser's hordes was to be seen and the whole proceedings were marked with patriotism, which amounted almost with reverence, which brought home to us all more than ever the unity of our vast and glorious Empire. Conspicuous among the wreckers were young girls, two of whom I spoke to. One had lost a father and a sister on the *Lusitania*, and the other a brother on the *Falaba*.

The following day Harry went ashore. The German Consulate had been wrecked and some other shops. The ship landed a body of marines in the evening as it was thought that the natives might start looting.

On the Saturday the ship left at 8am for Durban, and after coaling, picking up mail, and fresh supplies sailed to anchor at Walfish Bay where 5000 Union troops were now stationed. The camp held some German prisoners of war.

On the 9th June the *Armadale Castle* arrived bringing with her the new captain for the *K.C.* He was Commander T. Dannreuther. As soon as they were on board, and after picking up some of the prisoners, the ship sailed for Simons Town. On reaching Simons Town the prisoners were taken ashore and placed in a detention centre, and the ship went into dry dock.

Whilst in dock it was found the boilers were in a very poor condition, and several bottom plates had been buckled. The buzz around the ship was that this could mean the ship would be going home. However, coaling commenced, and after taking on 1100 hundred tons over two days, the *K.C.* went to sea again.

The captain held a meeting in the wardroom and told them that all the midshipmen would have to go to the East Coast again very shortly, their services being urgently required there for the whalers which were taking part in the operation which will be carried out next month. There are all kinds of rumours flying around the ship as regards future movements. Had she not had engine troubles the *K.C.* was to go to Australia (Fremantle) to escort Australian troops.

Friday 9th July. Princess Mary's Christmas gifts arrived yesterday from Zanzibar on the SS *Zanoi*. In the afternoon we had a whip round for a young sub lt who is marrying a young girl he met during the ship's stay in Durban. We bought him a gold sovereign case.

Forty of our men are forming a guard of honour for General Botha.

Harry's last day on *Kingsfaun Castle* proved to be on Tuesday 20th July 1915 whilst the ship was at Simons Town. He was hoping to go home, but the powers to be had other ideas.

THREE

JOINING THE WARDROOM

In February 1916, Sub. Lt. Harry C. Gaffney, for he had now gone from the gunroom to the wardroom, received a draft chit to the 1200 ton monitor H.M.S. *Severn*. She had been built by Vickers to be sold to Brazil, but in 1914 when war had been declared the Royal Navy had bought her. Two other monitors, the *Mersey* and the *Humber*, had also been built at this time and all saw service on Cape Station.

They were flat bottomed and totally unseaworthy in any kind of choppy weather. In 1915, the *Severn* had been towed to the Rufiji River Delta, via Malta, mainly because of her shallow draft of only five feet, and the heavy armament she carried.

She was armed with two 6-inch guns, two 4.7's and four 3-pounders which could be used as anti-aircraft guns.

Her captain, E. Fullerton D.S.O. Royal Navy, had married one of Lord Asher's daughters. He had previously been in command of H.M.S. *Swiftoe*, and been promoted to captain for his services on the Belgian coast.

The D.S.O. had been awarded for Rufiji River action. He had ten officers and a hundred men under his command.

He had an assortment of officers on board, R.N., R.N.R., and R.N.V.R. His navigator, Lt. Griffiths R.N. had been on the China Station at the outbreak of war, but had joined the *Severn* when the ship was at Chatham. Lt. Grenfell R.N.V.R. had been an instructor at the officer training establishment in Osborne, and had been given a commission on account of his knowledge of languages. He was also the official photographer. His engineer officer, Lt. Maclevel, was an R.N. officer who lived at Gillingham in Kent and also joined the ship at Chatham.

On Thursday 3rd February 1916 they were off the East African coast near Gaze. A couple of officers were landed to mark out positions for the *Severn* to bombard. They had to travel quite a way inland on foot and then clear some of the thick vegetation as it was obscuring the markers. Stationed closer to the shoreline was a British Army camp with 600 Indian troops, commanded by five British officers. It was an unhealthy place and malaria was rampant. The officers were constantly being replaced as one by one they came down with malaria.

Harry and the engineer left the ship in early February to visit the camp.

The Indian troops had just been in a skirmish with a German force, consisting of several hundred Askaris. These Askaris who served as the East African police were very pro-German and led by German officers. But when an Askari was captured by the British, they would often turn against their German officers and act as spies for the

British. One of the British officers had been wounded and fell into the enemy's hands.

They put the officer in a sack with his head showing, put him on the ground and jumped on him until he was almost dead. They then buried him in a vertical position with only his head showing above the ground, and left him there for the prowling hyenas!

During the next two weeks the British began to increase their troop strength. It was estimated at the time that the Germans had a force of 20,000 men, 5000 of which are German, the rest being native. The British force consisted of:

> Union troops – 12,000
> 2nd. Rhodesian Regt. – 2000
> Original IEF – 3000
> 40th Pathans and Baluchis – 2000
> Lancaster Fusiliers – 2500 + natives.

The build-up continued with troop ships arriving almost daily along the eastern coast. Bloody battles took place in all the German-held colonies. The *Severn* took every opportunity to bombard the coastal towns where German forces were encamped.

Tuesday 29th February at 7:45am the *Severn* had proceeded to a point off Vanga where she anchored head and stern and at 10:15 opened fire with both the 6-inch and the 4.7's at a camp three miles inland. The location of the camp being obtained from a German prisoner. At 10:45 the bombardment was over, and Harry notes in his logbook: My cabin was in a rather bad state after the firing as the concussion from the after 6 inch gun had smashed the wash stand, and brought everything on the sides down on the deck, much to the amusement of the others, and of course to my discomfort. However, it is all in a day's work.

Wednesday 1ˢᵗ March.

Weighed at 6am. Went to Vanga. After breakfast we sent our motor boats away to capture natives fishing in dugouts. They are not allowed to fish any lower down the coast than Gaze. They took the dugouts and the natives on board and the following day handed the lot over to the military authorities in Gaze. They then steamed south, and seeing some Askaris ashore fired the 3-pounder and scattered them.

On the 7ᵗʰ March they received a wireless message from Capt. Dickson. "Your shelling on the 29ᵗʰ appears to have been both effective and successful, as my reports inform me that all the trenches and huts of the Germans have been battered beyond recognition – huge batches of blood everywhere in the immediate surroundings. Up to the present it has not been ascertained the casualties of the enemy, but as their forces were concentrated at that point, it must be in the region of 600.

Severn continued to patrol the eastern coast for the next several weeks. Gun drill became the order of the day, with coaling every few days. It was a dreary routine. In June they received the news of the naval engagement off the Jutland Bank. Needless to say it caused a profound sensation of joy, alternating with sorrow so intense, to think of the terrible loss of life. The unfortunate circumstances that prevent our sharing of the task with our gallant comrades, and the favouring elements again siding with the enemy, thus preventing there complete destruction.

Late in June, whilst the ship was in Zanzibar, the troop ship *Dilwara* came into port. They had sixty Belgian officers amongst their passengers. They were going up country to join their forces. We had a lot of them on board in the morning and celebrated a regular entente. Most of them had been through all the phases of the war in Europe, and remembered the monitors off the coast. They all showed intense admiration for our army, especially the Scottish regiments.

At the end of the month, the captain granted some local leave, and a group of officers and matelots were invited to Prison Island. This doesn't sound much like a holiday resort, but my father's description of the place seems to suggest something of a tropical paradise. Staying in small villas, next to the beach he writes.

June 26 Monday till 29th

Lewis, myself, and a bunch of matelots and the company they picked themselves so that they could be with their own particular pals, to enjoy a time absolutely their own, and free of all restrictions. Left the ship after lunch for Prison Island.

In the 1900s when the prisoners had completed their work, it was made a quarantine station and a spot used by the forensic coterie for recuperative sojourns, being government prospects. The men live in a small bungalow, small only in a comparative sense. Facing the shore and a short distance removed from ours, which is spacious to the place of habitation – an old building has been converted into a temporary canteen whence emanates the odoriferous fumes of beer, whilst tins of indubitable delicacies stack the shelves, so that the matelots whilst relishing them, can afterwards then in a meditative mood over the pipe of solace, once again recall more vividly the dreams of home. The missing luxuries, however small, the rigid discipline of active service has thrust firmly effectively into but a background of reminiscence. They are enjoying it to the full and in quite the sportsman spirit. It would appear that this party comprises all the vocal talent in the ship, just as the stars creep forth rubbing their eyes, twinkling o'er head, as darkness silently steals across a placid sky, those refrains wafted towards us on the wings of the gentle breeze, synchronising and thus seemingly acknowledging, acquiescing to the mysterious ways of Nature, with criticisms devoid of austerity. How pleasing those harmonic sounds, rekindling the fires of ancient thoughts. If only for that, to live again the past!

This is a ravishing spot wherein the most exacting nature most irrevocably succumb to its charms – and then! Rest in perfect contentment, glorying in its beautiful endowment. Just a little islet! On one side fringed with coconut palms, with avenues of casuarinas like attendant courtiers – t'would indeed be simpler to say firs, as the difference I cannot detect, and it would give you a better impression.

As I gaze on this scene – with these varying degrees of life, yet sacred to all, my heart was full of generous homage for these creatures. The birds that sung so sweetly, giving inspirations for mortal song, so that over appreciation gratitude is solely for our kinfolk.

The Egrets sought for its decorative sprays to assuage the whims and capriciousness of women deep in vanity. To earn largess for man.

The startled gazelles who fear their bodies for an empty larder. Their horns the trophies of a materialistic chase. I wanted to tell them my thoughts, to allay their suspicions, groundless in one poor soul. To thank them for their past in this great life pageant.

Yet how could I make them understand me? I wandered on! Thinking this world more topsy-turvy than ever. So many living things. Whilst all the sad world needs, is just the art of being kind.

Then the quaintest little cemetery, midst dreamy magnolia blossoms, under a canopy of firs, immobile spectators. Sphinx-like sentinels, shedding their broom as the seasons come and go (like tears of the mourners for the demise). So that now the deep rich russet brown of maturity replaces the adolescent green o'er the surface of this graveyard by the sea. Like departing day its scenic grandeur – unpaintable, but never forgotten.

As I write from the veranda of the bungalow I cannot but help think what a worthy vista we must make to this picturesque façade. A beach of soft dry sand washed by the turquoise waters dazzling, basking in the sun, their revelry but accentuating their scintillation, and further on two small islands – green specks, seemingly lying at the foot of the mainland, whose slopes, resplendent with the numerous clove groves and other plants, just skirting its shores an old palace, almost neglected, so that decay and ruin prove to be buy the sole remaining attraction is to an interesting past. Through the tree before me, as their boughs and shimmering leaves perpetually sway in the breeze. A far eastern town is discernible, exaggerated, distorted in architectural vulgarity by the mirage.

He finishes with: Just this brief holiday as we are leaving now but it has been magnificent. I do not purpose to eulogise further, but this description I think shows that the materialistic veneer unconsciously cultivated, is indeed but superficial.

The last party arrived back from Prison Island at dusk. They were a party of stokers and had somewhat abused the privileges given them in their drunken orgies, by breaking some of the gear lent to us. They had, very righteously, angered the captain who, after telling them some home truths, set them on repairing the damage. Regrettably the officers all suffered from this outburst and were put on sea watches. Shortly after the *Severn* sailed for the port of Tanga. The war news was becoming much better. The British forces now approaching Tanga. The normal population of this seaport had been 20,000 of which 200 were white. This had dwindled considerably; the latter number were represented by a few Greeks and Germans of no military significance. After having given their parole they were all lodged in one of the larger houses. The place almost everywhere bore traces of naval bombardments which it had been subjected to. The most damage being done to the pier and the adjacent warehouses. In the bay the steamer *Markgraff* lies on her side, being alternately awash and high and dry with the tide.

The impression one receives on approaching Tanga from seaward is a town built on a small and low plateau, amongst coconut groves and mango trees, which with the exception of the spacious and handsome hospital, the British Mission and a few small villas, conceals the major portion of the town. In Market Square, around the Bismarck monument are seven unexploded 12-inch lyddite shells, with smaller fragments belonging to shells of a smaller calibre.

As we walked along Market Street, bon St. Paul St. it was indeed hard to realise that twenty months ago much British blood was lost in attempting the capture of the town. The Royal North Lancs. and the Gurkhas had shown indomitable courage capturing the railway station with fearful losses. What a pity those brave sons of Lancashire and those dusky soldiers from the hills of Nepal were not here to enter first in triumph.

The following month (July) the *Severn* entered Pangani Harbour, the town having been captured by the 57th Rifles. Whilst anchored in the harbour a dog swam from the shore and climbed on board. As Harry had spotted it first, he claimed it. It remained with him for the rest of the time he was on the *Severn*. It was not the only addition the ship received as the Army authorities brought a captured German officer aboard. The natives ashore had been instructed to light a fire on the beach should German troops arrive. That night, seeing a fire on the beach, the *Severn* opened fire. However, the Germans had set fire to the village and left the village before the *Severn* had opened fire.

The following day (1st August) at 7am the Union Jack was hoisted over the Boma-Goothouse, with no opposition having been experienced. Though later in the day much sniping went on, which resulted in one soldier and one officer being wounded.

The German officer was living in the wardroom so that the officers could get information out of him. He spoke English fluently having lived in Montreal for several years. Curiously the ship had chased him all down the coast: firstly he had escaped us at Ullenge, fired at us from the shore whilst we seized Jambe Island, just cleared out in time from Tanga, come under fire at Tangata, left Paangani just before we occupied it. Then finally ran to earth here.

The prisoner told them that at the attack on Tanga, the night our transports arrived they had put 148 troops in the town during the night they received 1100 reinforcements from the north. During our attack they had fallen back to their last line of trenches, and were about to evacuate the place, when to their surprise the British troops had fallen back. They had seventy killed, but the British casualties were a staggering 800. He had personally buried sixty-four Tommies that had been felled by one Maxim gun.

Harry concluded from his conversations with him that he was a particularly broad-minded person, yet still had implicit faith in everything his government advocated. He did admit that the British treated their prisoners of war far better than they did.

The next day they transferred the prisoner to the *Mersey* but Harry kept his dog.

In mid-August it was Captain Fullerton's last day aboard the *Severn*. The wardroom gave him a party, and presented him with a silver salver with a ship engraved and signed by all the officers. The following day he was rowed ashore by his officers in a last gesture of respect.

The new incoming skipper, Lt. Cmdr. Jones, gathered the wardroom together, and gave them a situation report.

On the 16th August the *Severn* arrived off Msasani Bay at 3am. As the dawn broke they closed the shore. The shore side batteries opened fire on the *Severn*. The firing was so accurate that shells were exploding all around the *Severn*. They were ordered to retire.

Harry notes in his log book: this is the first time I have been under big gun fire at long range. It is a weird sensation. First, the flash from the enemy guns, the optimist in the fore top (the fire control station) shouts out the number of incoming shells. Then a wait of two seconds, which of course varies according to the range, then a thunderous noise overhead. Then it's either a plonk in the water, or on board. (If you are fortunate the former.) We were. But I should have liked one or two on board in a non-vital place to witness the effects. The lyddite or TNT shells leave a dullish green colour in the water for some little time afterwards. H.M.S. *Vengeance* bombarded Dar es Salaam with troop train be it the former!

The *Vengeance* leaves today for Bombay for dry dock and then she is going to the Eastern Mediterranean.

In October 1916, Harry, still serving aboard the *Severn*, was made a temporary gun lt. and because they were very short handed in the wardroom, Harry had also taken on the duties of navigator, having lost two officers who had been sent to hospital with malaria.

They were still patrolling up and down the east coast of Africa and by month's end they anchored off Dar es Salaam. General Smuts had arrived on station to take charge of all British troops.

But it was not all work and no play.

The wardroom had invited the matron and six nurses from the South Africa General Hospital to a party on board. It evidently was most successful as Harry then invited one of them to a moonlight picnic. The following month on November 11th it was Harry's twenty-third birthday, and he records he took Sister L for a picnic. The last ever entry records that he and another fellow officer took Sisters L and E for a picnic. Most enjoyable time.

FOUR

NORE COMMAND, CHATHAM

In the early part of 1917 Harry reported to Chatham Barracks to be drafted to H.M.S. *Fervent*, berthed at Chatham Dockyard. The *Fervent* was part of the Nore Defence Flotilla. It was only the smaller ships of the Navy which could navigate the eight miles along the marshy and narrow river banks of the Medway.

Chatham Dockyard employed 10,000 skilled artisans at that time, with its many dry docks, basins, foundries, workshops, and boat slips. Materials were transported between these buildings by its own steam locomotive. It was the number one employer of the hustling, bustling seaport. In the course of its history it had built over 500 ships for the Navy; the most famous one was of course Admiral Lord Nelson's flagship, H.M.S. *Victory*, launched in 1765.

The mast ponds in the dockyard were used for seasoning the fir logs by immersing them in saltwater to get the sap out of them. The desk that has stood in the Oval Office since 1880 at Washington D.C. was made from timbers that were seasoned in the Chatham

Dockyard mast ponds. The planks used for the desk originally came from H.M.S. *Resolute*.

Harry (with pipe) on the bridge

Fervent was one of only two ships built of this class, the other being H.M.S. *Zephyr*. They were the forerunners to the destroyers of the future. They weighed 320 tons fully loaded, had a length of 204 feet, and were armed with one 12-pounder and two torpedo tubes. Initially they were fitted with locomotive boilers, with one funnel, but could not reach the contracted speed. The Admiralty then ordered them to be fitted with Reed Boilers, with four funnels. These boilers produced 4000iph, giving them a speed of 26 knots. She had a crew of fifty-three.

It was whilst on board H.M.S. *Fervent* that the twenty-year-old Harry went missing from his ship. The Commander G from Chatham reported to the admiral that Lt. Gaffney was missing.

Many years later I obtained his war records from the National Archives in London which showed Harry had got married in the law courts in Natal, Durban to a Miss Evelyn Doreen Livingstone on January 24th 1918. At this time nobody in the family knew of this, and after returning to England at war's end, the family were none too pleased to hear about it. They applied so much pressure on him that Harry was made to divorce Evelyn.

Harry was to spend a year on board H.M.S. *Fervent*, before being drafted to H.M.S. Sligo as the navigating officer, *Sligo* was part of the 7th Fast Minesweeping Flotilla which swept the east coast of England and the North Sea area. Another year later saw him reporting to H.M.S. *Gladious*, a fleet sweeping sloop of the Arabis class. She weighed in at 1250 tons and was a coal burner having a top speed of 16 knots. They swept off both the east and west coasts of Scotland, the Orkney, and Shetland Islands.

Later in that year my father received his first command at twenty-four years of age. He was appointed C.O. of Torpedo boat No. 20. Also of the Nore Defence Flotilla operating out of Chatham.

It was about this time that my father became involved with politics. He was invited to stand as a parliamentary candidate for the National Party, eventually absorbed by the Unionist Party. He received permission from the Admiralty to address ratings and others at Sheerness and Chatham Dockyards on behalf of Havelock Wilson's campaign for adequate compensation for merchant seamen and dependants who had lost their lives due to enemy submarine action. He was also involved in working on clauses for various peace treaties.

On the 30th November 1919, Harry was finally demobbed from the Navy. He had been at sea for the best part of eight years starting with the sailing barque *Inversnaid* before the war.

But he did not stay away from the sea for long. The following year in 1920, he, and a group of fellow wartime officers, who had served with him in Chatham, founded the Coastal Carrying Corporation. They collectively purchased an auxiliary/sailing ship and named her the *Admiral Keyes*.

She was a three-masted schooner of wooden construction. She had been built by G. Stenback in Kristinestad, Finland and was fitted with an engine and a single screw. Weighing 250 tons, she was light in the water, although her measurements of 118 feet in length, and a draft of 11 feet, made her quite a big vessel.

Listed in the Lloyds Register of Sailing Ships in 1920/1921, my father (Harry C. Gaffney) is recorded as Manager of the CCC with the ship's official number listed as 144304.

The captain, elected by his fellow officers, was Lt. Commander Thompson who had been the CO of the paddle minesweeper H.M.S. *Newbury* who had won the Distinguish Service Cross and Bar for saving his ship, that had been set on fire by a German destroyer squadron. My father's eldest son, Jeremy, told me that the five officers from the Navy that joined father in this venture were a motley crowd resembling a bunch of pirates who never had a penny between them.

What happened next can be read in the *Times* newspaper dated 14th May 1920. It reported:

It was on this day that whilst under weigh from London to Falmouth the *Admiral Keyes* sprang a leak and had to be towed into Dover harbour to be unloaded. It was shortly after leaving Dover that she sank. Jeremy is fully convinced that this was due to a decided interest in insurance money rather than a lack of seamanship skills. Be that as it may it was the end of the CCC.

Father was now at a loose end and like many seafaring people found it difficult to settle into civilian life. He held various jobs between the wars, one of which was Director and Secretary for the British Ship Owners (Sailing) Association, and was employed at another time as publicity manager for a commercial film company. He was also owner of a demolition company, and part owner of a racehorse, although my research has not found anything about the horses he may have owned.

FIVE

HISTORY REPEATS ITSELF

In 1939, at the outbreak of war, Harry re-joined the Royal Navy as a temporary Lt. and was drafted to H.M.S. Marmiom of the 12th Minesweeping Flotilla based on the River Clyde. The Marmiom and her sister ships of the Flotilla were coal-burning, paddle-wheeled ships. They were opened bridge with a canvas screen wrapped around the lower part of the bridge.

The war had taken a turn for the worse in Europe for the Allies and in late May 1940, it reached a point where the British, French, and Belgian armies had been driven back to the beaches at Dunkirk. Over 300,000 troops were now stranded, backed up to the sea, and every available ship in Britain, or indeed anything that could safely cross the Channel, was called upon to rescue these troops and bring them back across the Channel to safety. 800 boat owners responded to the call.

The 12th Minesweeping Flotilla at the time consisted of H. M. Ships Waverley, Duchess of Fife, Oriole, Goatfell, and Marmiom, which were off the coast at Yarmouth, and after coaling were ordered to cross the Channel to La Panne a few miles from Dunkirk.

Duchess of Kent, Princess Marina of Denmark and Greece,
leaving H.M.S. *Goatfell*, escorted by her Co, Lt. Commander
Harry Cecil Gaffney.

On the 29th May 1940 H.M.S. *Marmion* lowered her
lifeboats and picked up survivors from a mined French
transport and transferred them to a French destroyer.
She then picked up over 300 British and French troops
and sailed for Dover. After disembarking the troops there
she returned to the beaches in Dunkirk and picked up a
further 200 soldiers. Over head the Luftwaffe were strafing
the beaches and continued bombing the ships all the way
across the Channel. The *Marmiom*, on her third and final
trip, and having rescued over 700 troops, returned, this
time to the port of Harwich. Sadly after a few days tied up
alongside in Harwich a German bomber scored a direct
hit on the *Marmiom*. The bomb went straight through the
upper deck, down through all the other decks and out
the bottom plates, sending her to a watery grave. It was a
shallow grave which left her masts and funnel poking out

of the water. There were no casualties, and although she was raised, she was later sent for scrap.

My father had been promoted to Lt. Commander and in April 1942 was drafted to another paddle minesweeper, H.M.S. *Goatfell*, that had been requisitioned for the duration of the war. Formerly she had been the *Caledonia* of the Caledonia Steam Packet Company. When my father joined her she was part of the 11th Minesweeping Flotilla based on the Thames where they were undergoing conversion to anti-aircraft vessels, known as eagle ships. On completing her conversion *Goatfell* arrived in Sheerness on the 16th May, having suffered extensive damage from splinters during one of the air raids on London on the night of the 10th/11th May.

She was ordered to the *Humber* as AA ship. She was armed with one 12-pounder, two pom-poms, four Boulton Paul turrets, two Hotchkiss guns, two 303 Lewis guns, and two depth charge chutes. Whilst in the *Humber* she had a number of engagements with enemy aircraft. On the night of 26 Feb. 1942 she shot down a Junkers 88, which had attempted to attack the *Humber* light float, and damaged another, which was probably lost.

Harry spent another few months on the *Humber*, but then was sent to the United States to pick up a newly launched Landing Ship (Tanks).

LST 364

Harry and his future crew sailed to New York on the SS *Queen Mary* which was acting as a troop ship at that time.

The *Queen Mary* sailed as part of a convoy, and after a safe passage docked in New York.

The future crew of LST 364. were accommodated on the other side of the Hudson River in two New Jersey hotels. These hotels, named The New Monterey and The Berkly Carteret were taken over by the Navy and renamed H.M.S. Asbury.

These ships (LSTs), and there were many built in the war, were known as Long Slow Targets by the crews that manned them.

LST 364 was an American-built landing craft which was transferred to the Royal Navy for the duration of the war under the Lend-Lease arrangement with the U.S. in the bases for ships deal. My father joined her on the 20th October 1942, six days before she was launched in Quincy, Mass. On December 7th she was officially handed over to the Royal Navy. My father took over command with a crew of nine officers, and a 120 ratings. There was additional accommodation for fourteen officers and 131 troops. She was heavily armed with two twin Bofors, and twelve single 20 mm gun mounts, and had a cargo capacity of 1650 tons, and had an extraordinary endurance being able to travel 24,000 miles at 9 knots, whilst displacing 3960 tons. They were notoriously bad sea ships as they were flat bottomed, with a shallow draught. The blunted bow did not help matters.

She sailed from New York on March 17th 1943 as a straggler in convoy UGS-6A. By June 1943 LST 364 was in Alexandria preparing for the North African and Sicilian landings. On July 19th my father sent the following memo to the troops on board. It read:

Will you please convey to our comrades in arms soon to disembark from this ship, what a very great pleasure their presence has given us and, while not unmindful of their wonderful past advances, we shall look forward with supreme confidence to their future victories – wherever and whenever you see us come on board. You will always be welcomed.

Lt. Cmdr. H.C. Gaffney. R.N.R.

To which the C.O. of the troops replied:

On behalf of all Army personnel on board this ship, I wish to convey to you, your officers and ratings, our very great thanks for the kindness and consideration you have shown us.

You have done everything that it has been possible to do to help us, and make life on board as comfortable as possible, and we appreciate this. Rest assured that we will not forget the Royal Navy, and especially LST 364.

O.C. The Durham Light Infantry.

My father reports of what was to follow.

My Sicilian campaign, which really commenced when we left Bougie (North Africa) early in June 1943 for Alexandria, leaving that port on the 23rd with embarked 8th Army personnel, their heavy guns and mechanical equipment arriving at Tripoli at the end of the month, sailing from there in time to reach the beaches at first light on D day the 10th July. This, in terms of voyages.

Alexandria-Tripoli-Marina Avola (Sicily).
Marina Avola-Malta. Embarking Gen. Eisenhower's car at Sousse (North Africa).

Sousse-Marina-Avola-Sousse.

Sousse-Syracuse-

Sousse-Augusta (east coast of Sicily) three times.

Augusta-Panterilla-Souse.

Reduced to figures, it shows:

    1) Distance covered 7000 miles.

    2) Troops carried, 3000.

    3) Tanks, guns, motor transports, 750.

We were then sent to Ferryville, the French naval base on the lake of Bizetta for a ten-day rest and refit. Bizetta is a shambles, and as you enter the small harbour and pass down the narrow natural canal about seven miles long before entering the lake, plenty of headaches await you. There are at least a dozen wrecks, some above water, and some submerged. Going in for the first time with no knowledge of them I gave myself a couple of S-bends when one would have been enough. There were plenty of anxious moments as it was getting dark; negotiating the first one, some helpful voice bawled out through a loud hailer from the signal tower, "Do you know the Channel?" This I have added to my famous last words.

I have omitted the fact that before we arrived at this stage, we had been at anchor for two days in the outer bay, when each night we had two unpleasant raids lasting about an hour. The first occasion we had two bombs very close to us. The flak was terrific, the search lights were good. I had never seen so many planes held in the beams for so long a period, or so many planes diving down the beams in their avoiding action. Eight were claimed and credited on the first night, and three on the second.

Just before the end of the war LST 364 returned to the United Kingdom. At 0245 on the 22nd February 1945 she was sailing off the Margate Roads at the tail end of convoy T.A.M. 87 at 8 knots. Three hours later she was struck by a torpedo dropped from a German Heinkel 111. At the time she was fully loaded with troops, tanks, lorries, and twelve half-ton amphibious tract vehicles bound for Ostend.

The ship was struck on the starboard quarter. The hole was from the upper deck to below the water line and thirty-five feet wide. Damage was extensive. The ship came to a standstill as the main bulkhead to the engine room had been fractured, and quickly flooded the engine room. The fire main had been split wide open, and rendered it inoperable, thus eliminating the most important option of the ship's firefighting equipment. Fires broke out all over the ship and many of the vehicles, which had been set ablaze, caused minor explosions. By this time the tank deck was rapidly flooding and the vehicles were submerged. At the same time, petrol continued to burn on top of the water.

The crew left with only portable fire extinguishers, attempted to put out the fires on the upper deck, but found that even when successful, the fires would often reignite.

In the meantime H.M. Trawler *Turquoise*, one of the escorting vessels of the convoy was signalled to come alongside and take off the wounded. LST 364 was settling stern first at an alarming rate. The captain realised he had little chance of saving his ship, and requested the *Turquoise* to take the whole ship's company aboard, which they did. Miraculously there was no loss of life aboard the LST 364 although there were thirty casualties.

For the remainder of the day and night the stern remained submerged with the bows sticking out of the water. In the morning of the following day, 23rd Feb. 1945, H.M.S. *Rutherford* was sent out to sink her by gunfire. LST 364 now lies on the bottom at 120 feet. May she rest in peace.

In his report at the official enquiry the captain praised the crew for the remarkable way in which they handled the situation. "It was in the best traditions of the Navy," he said.

LST. 199

The next morning at eleven, Harry was sent for and told that he had to rush up to Bizerta and take command of LST 199. She had been built at the Chicago Bridge and Iron Company site at Seneca situated on the River Illinois. Work on building the yard did not start until 1st May 1942; however, Seneca launched its first ship LST 197 on the 13th December 1942. Less than two months later LST 199 was launched.

Very quickly the Company developed the 'Task System' for building LSTs. A total of 378 tasks, comprising 114 operations were required for each ship. Ship construction time was divided into twenty equal periods. The ship was on land during the first eighteen work periods, and the last two periods were completed when she was waterborne. Each ship required in the region of 30,000 parts, six-and-a-half miles of piping system, thirteen miles of electrical cable, and approximately 130 motors. The cellular construction of the hull consisted of three tiers of box sections 10 feet wide and about 24 feet long on each side of the ship. There were forty-eight of these box sections to a ship, those for the Seneca ships being fabricated in Chicago, Greenville (Pennsylvania) and Birmingham, Alabama. They were shipped to Seneca on railway flat trucks.

In May 1944 the yard produced nine ships, one in every three-and-one-half days! This meant a seventy-hour week for all employees.

Five shipbuilding yards had to be created on the inland waterways of the Rivers Ohio and Illinois for the construction of the LSTs, as all other shipbuilding yards were stretched to capacity. Known collectively as the 'Cornfield shipyards', they were: Seneca (Illinois), Ambridge (Pennsylvania), Jeffersonville (Indiana), Evansville (Indiana), and the Dravo yard at Neville Island (Pennsylvania). The U.S. Maritime Commission shows that a total 1152 LSTs were built, of these 670 were built on the inland water yards.

Harry was on board LST 199 within the hour with his shaving gear and another change of tropical kit. Another hour later he had to move the ship and oil immediately. She was already loaded with American troops, and found out the first C.O. had had a nervous breakdown, and his replacement had only been on board for one day when he had a heart attack. He certainly looked ghastly when I turned up. They got him ashore, and immediately left for Augusta. Upon arrival there we discharged the troops and vehicles and went out into the harbour to anchor. The date now being 26th August.

We averaged three daylight raids until 2nd September, and one each night. Apart from two near-misses, and almost choked by our own smoke (we have a special smoke-making machine), we escaped unscathed.

On the 2nd Sept. we went up the coast to Cantania (Sicily) and loaded up with Canadian troops, motor transport and guns and returned to Augusta in the evening. There was an opportunity to go ashore. The harbour here is of moderate size, with one or two wrecks around, but there was no attempt to block the entrance. The waterfront has received a good battering. The town seemed scattered and spread around the bay, but in a reasonable condition, which is overshadowed from the north by the towering Etna. Upon returning from Augusta we were briefed and learned we were to leave in two groups of twelve in the early hours for Reggio. It was a dark night, or morning, as we left at 0100, 3rd August and we all cleared the boom with relief, and commenced our sixty-mile journey up the coast keeping well inshore.

We had been told that the shore batteries were opening the show with a two-hour bombardment across the Straits of Messina. In the little time we had to ruminate before our departure, there being a lot of plans, photos, and general instructions to absorb, we wondered what sort of reception we could expect. The general opinion was that with a high ground on the mainland we could expect the beaches to be shelled, plus a few air attacks. At first light, we made our point on the coast and commenced our dash across the Straits, a distance of about four miles. There was still the flash and rumble of our big guns as they pounded the now silent defences, who were dropping shells ahead of us, waiting for us to run into them. They evidently could only train these guns on certain bearings, otherwise they could not have failed to hit us.

As we were being signalled to our various beaches we had a sharp air attack. It was a tense few moments, a few bombs, one or two near-misses and all was quiet. Here we found the ideal beach.

Harry then took the ship towards the beach at full speed. He reports: It was an exhilarating feeling as we let the stern anchor go, and with the cable free, rushed forward to the sand ahead. The giant bow doors opened, parting the water on each side of the ship, driving it onward to the shore like a miniature tidal wave. The beach party now scattered in all directions, for as one of them told me later:

"I thought the ship would never stop." Then the climax as she mounts the beach and as it seems to me on the bridge, ever so gently. (The folks in the engine room have other ideas.) The platform, or as we call it the ramp (15 tons in weight), is lowered and discharge is started. The tank, or hold as it would be called in a merchant ship, soon gets empty. Then the upper deck at the fore end and there is a big elevator which lowers the vehicles etc. down onto the tank deck and then they run out over the ramp as the others have done. Eighty minutes is a quick time, a great deal depends on the types you have and how they are beached.

Our mission is to run night and day between these beaches and San Theresa, which is sixteen miles on the Sicilian side. So off we go in the middle of the Straits, we are attacked by five fighter bombers, who come at us from the sun and drop bombs all around us. It's all over in seconds. The noise of the planes, the swish of the bombs, the explosion, this is a close shave, and on we go. We are getting enquiries from ships in the distance if all is well, so we beach on the other side and commence loading all over again. Here things are taking a few hours. The beach is good but there is little surf, which results in having to keep the engines running to keep the ship on the beach. This is an irksome business and means no spell. We do this for four days and nights, averaging three hours' sleep, when you can, or how you can.

We are blessed with the bluest skies and beaming sun. On our second trip across, and whilst we were discharging, a motor launch secured alongside. I noticed a 'Duck' alongside her which slowly waddled its way to the beach and then ashore, where one or two cameramen were taking pictures of it. So I dashed ashore, via the tank deck and ramp to find General Montgomery, a tall, lean man with a sun-baked face. He might have been taken for a Texan, complete with his black beret, and his right hand extended in his accustomed manner, as he passed soldiers congregated on the beach. I thought it imitative and theatrical.

The Straits are now one mass of all types of landing craft, with the Ducks making an almost continuous line across. These amphibious craft (Ducks) carry two-and-a-half tons, and it is a strange sight to see them come out of the water, change over to land propulsion with their propeller high and dry astern. It's even quainter to see them come in from the sea, mount our ramp, and park themselves in the tank deck. One of the successes of the war.

During our absence there had been another quick raid along the beaches. Prisoners were coming in and being embarked in smaller craft. Had an opportunity for a quick glance at Reggio Harbour, which seemed to have plenty of wrecks inside. No attempt to use it whilst we were there.

During the course of our bombardment, 150,000 shells were fired across the Straits. We had so many LSTs and smaller landing craft that the loading was slowed down considerably, though the stuff was pouring across the other side in an endless stream. We did four trips all together. We had carried 400 vehicles, and 2000 troops.

At midnight we were ordered to proceed, only the leader knowing our destination. It was a very dark night as we weighed and headed northward. It soon started to rain, which reduced visibility to a few yards. Then one of the most violent thunderstorms with vivid and blinding lightening reduced the visibility to almost zero. I had no oilskin with me and just stood there dripping with glasses glued to my eyes trying to keep station. Mercifully, as we approached the narrows the storm abruptly abated with the rain, well just rain not a cascade. This was just as well as the straits of Messina at this point are narrowed to less than a couple of miles, with odd whirlpools and a fast-moving current making navigation difficult under normal circumstances. We were negotiating without any lights or buoys when we were halfway through we found a small convoy of landing craft approaching us, southbound. There was almost complete chaos, for at this point we were all altering course. The whole scene was at once illuminated momentarily by a balloon, which had been struck by lightning. I think all concerned deserve full marks, and all certainly heaved a sigh of relief when we finally cleared the Straits without casualties. The possibility of a marine rodeo were plenty. This was without doubt one of the most anxious nights I have had on this ship, the other being in February off Cape May.

At that time we had just arrived in the small port of Termini, twenty miles east of Palermo. We loaded up with American troops, all their guns, and equipment. We loaded their 'long Toms' and all the other armament. At 2200 whilst we were being briefed in LST 425, which was alongside us, we heard a heavy crump and thought a raid had started. However, it transpired that a solitary torpedo plane had come in with lights on, and torpedoed LST 417. Twelve of her ships company had been killed. Our present doctor had been the first on board and tended to the other casualties. We had to beach her, and unload her cargo and troops.

It was whilst aboard LST 199 that Harry was promoted to commander.

The last days of the 199 were to be in the Java Sea, just off Surabaya. It was November 1945 when she was struck by a mine on the port quarter. Although severely damaged the crew saved her from sinking. She was towed back to harbour and left high and dry on the beach, her ship's company being drafted to other ships of the Pacific fleet.

LST 415

My father left LST 364 on the 10th April 1944 when she docked at Casablanca and took command of LST 415 which was in dry dock for a ten-day refit. Norman Drew, the Jack Dusty on 415, remembers my father clearing lower deck, and telling the crew that he would allow them as much leave as he could during the refit as they would probably not get any kind of leave after that.

Another member of the crew was able seaman Neville Magson, who was one of a family of nine from Yorkshire. He had commissioned the 415 in Baltimore, Maryland in the United States and remembers the ship being loaded with, amongst many other things, lard and baked beans destined for the Russians. Bound for the Med. LST 415 was to be involved with the North Africa, Sicily, and Italian campaigns. Neville was still aboard for the Normandy landings, and made many return trips back to the beaches. They brought back heavy equipment, tanks, lorries, and more troops. They also brought wounded Allied soldiers and German prisoners of war back to the English shores. Neville's time aboard LST 415 came to an end when she was torpedoed leaving the Thames Estuary bound for Ostend.

On completion of the refit, French troops, who had seen action in Anzio, were embarked with all their vehicles.

On the 21st April LST 415 left Casablanca and sailed for the U.K., arriving in Swansea on the 2nd May where she unloaded the French troops and their tanks. She then sailed for Gosport to prepare for the biggest invasion force that had ever been assembled. On June 5th 1944 she left Gosport fully loaded with troops and tanks as part of Operation Neptune. She arrived at Juno Beach near Couselles, Normandy around twelve noon on the 6th June 1944.

Assisting the landing craft flotilla were two British battleships, H.M.S. *Warspite*, a veteran ship from the Battle of Jutland in the First World War, and H.M.S. *Ramillies*. Both ships now heavily bombarded the beaches and neutralised the German guns on Juno Beach as LST 415 followed behind, and then landed their troops.

Just seven months after LST 415 hit the beaches at Normandy on D-Day 6th June 1944, and after many return trips to the beaches to bring home wounded British soldiers, and German prisoners of war, LST 415 was leaving Tilbury Docks, fully loaded with army vehicles and tanks as part of the British Liberation Army. Soldiers from the Highland Light Infantry were also on board. Her captain had stationed her last in the convoy, and was heading for the open sea for Ostend. As the ship proceeded off Southend into the North Sea, a German U-boat fired a salvo of torpedoes at her, one of which struck the port quarter, and the other amidships, instantly killing all the engine room crew. The ship came to a shuddering halt, and the soldiers on board mustered at their boat stations on deck. Watertight doors were quickly shut, which kept the ship afloat although the stern was partially submerged. LST 159 came alongside, and in total darkness, the soldiers leapt from the sloping deck of 415 onto the 159. Many left their weapons and equipment behind and in the scramble to leave the ship jumped into the sea, and fell between the two ships, and were squashed.

John Bessford, one of four cooks aboard her, had been aboard her for the Sicily and Italian landings at Reggio, Salano, and Anzio the same time as my father. He had also been aboard her for D-Day on the 6th June landings at Normandy. John always slept in a clean pair of overalls. His action station was the forward oerlikon cannon up in the bows of the ship. He ran forward to his gun in the darkness. He could see all kinds of horizontal tracer coming from the other ships, and although he could not see the target, knew it must be a surface one. Later he was a stretcher bearer, assisting in removing the fatalities from the ship when she eventually arrived at Rotherhide.

SIX

FLYING OVER THE
WAVES

Jeremy was born on the 24th November 1921 and was my father's second son. On the very few times he had contact with his father he seemed concerned he was a civilian. This was in October 1940. His father, Harry, had re-joined the Navy and was constantly at sea. One day Jeremy received a call from him telling him to report to one of the shipping managers based at one of the docks in London, as he was confident he could get me to sea as a 'deckhand'. At that time the shipping losses were very high, and the thought of volunteering for this nightmare was not appealing. However, such was the discipline in those days between father and son that he made his way with a heavy heart to a damaged dockside in London. This was no mean feat as public transport was minimal, but eventually he located a man housed in a broken down shed. He asked Jeremy several technical questions, particularly about his sailing experience on my father's yacht (a few hours with my younger brother Desmond on a rowing boat in the River Deben whilst on holiday). After about a half-hour he told Jeremy to "push off".

In October 1940 Jeremy had a job in a large London department store. In the evenings he was part of the local Defence Force, satirised many years later on television as *Dad's Army*. At the start the organisation was short of everything. They drilled with broomsticks in their civilian gear, and it was not until early 1941 before they received a uniform. They were issued with an American rifle, plus five rounds of ammo. Captain Watson, ex Royal Marines who was extremely strict, commanded the platoon that Jeremy was in.

One of the strategic posts was a small pillbox at the edge of Croydon Airport, between the main road and the factory estate. On one occasion a particularly heavy attack dropped several bombs on the Bourjois perfume factory only a hundred yards from our position.

With little sleep between the two jobs, he always felt tired. This routine continued until February 1942, when on his twentieth birthday he received his call-up papers from the Navy.

This was the start of a frantic series of intense instructional courses at various shore bases stretching over a period of twelve months. Besides seamanship, he was to do a lot of flying in Proctors, Lysanders, and Albacores to practice radio and visual communications. There was also gunnery practice on the 303 Lewis machine gun operated by the chap in the rear seat of Fairy Swordfish Mk.1.

By February 1943 Jeremy was a qualified telegraphist air gunner (TAG) for the Fleet Air Arm and as such was the only ratings allowed to fly. Pilots, observers, and navigators were officers.

At the end of his course he was sent to join a Fleet Requirement Unit based in Crail, Scotland. The duties of the FRU squadron were extremely varied. One moment it could be target-towing for a cruiser, at other times you could be dive bombing specific ships, or shore batteries of anti-aircraft guns. It was quite exhilarating to fly out to the target at wave top height, though not always easy to find the ship on the way back. Jeremy was never happy when on dive bombing exercises with his commanding officer. He would climb to 10,000 feet, put the plane into a vertical angle and dive for the ground. Sitting in the back, you were diving so steeply you saw over the head. At the last moment he would pull on the stick and the plane would shudder upright. The 'G' rating was excessive, often reaching over 7G.

In May 1943, whilst on a defence exercise at the base, he was detailed off to be the wireless operator in a square-boxed-shape, open-topped armour car, really a four-sided hunk of half-inch iron driven by an RAF mechanic. They were meant to be defending the base. Jeremy was standing up with the headphones on beside a huge radio. They were firing rockets, and laying all kinds of smokescreens, when the armoured car turned over. He was thrown upside down; the heavy transmitter fell on his face knocking out several teeth. When the armoured car finally stopped on the concrete runway he tried to get out but his hand was trapped underneath with the full weight of the vehicle on it. Several people tried to pull him out, including the C.O., but failed. Eventually a doctor crawled underneath and gave him some morphine. A crane arrived on the scene and lifted the armoured car clear. Jeremy was taken to the cottage hospital in Crail, but transferred from there to the naval hospital in Queensferry, near Edinburgh where he had his thumb and the back of his head stitched up.

At the end of December 1943, Jeremy was transferred to Lee on Solent. After a month there he was sent to a frontline squadron, No.835 which was aboard H.M.S. *Chaser*, but by the time he had reached there the squadron had been flown aboard H.M.S. *Audacity*.

The *Audacity* was one of the latest escort carriers to be built. Unlike the American carriers she had an iron flight deck whereas the Americans had built their carriers with wooden flight decks. They were to find out later in the war that this was a mistake that had huge consequences.

The *Audacity* had been built at the famous John Brown shipyard and had a displacement of 14,000 tons. It was just over 500 feet in length, but only 68 feet wide which was only 7 or 8 feet wider than the Swordfish which she carried. Her total complement consisted of nine Swordfish, and four Supermarine Sea Fires, which were to be replaced later by Wildcats.

The *Audacity* had been waiting for Jeremy and his crew as replacements to bring the squadron up to full strength. So a day after Jeremy joined the *Audacity* she steamed down the Clyde. It was his first seagoing experience, and he found it very strange, and as he later recalled it took some time to get used to. The next evening he was to experience his first take off which he found so nerve-racking that he doesn't remember a thing about it. In his next flight, after being airborne for half an hour, and after plenty of activity on the radio, the observer reported they were lost. Jeremy tried to get a bearing of the ship, but found he could not turn on the transmitter. He frantically played with the switches in front of him, but to no avail. Nothing in his courses that he had done had prepared him for this eventuality. However, some time later, when they were desperately short of fuel, they saw some tiny lights and they came into land. It was not the *Audacity*, but the RAF station at West Freugh! They stayed the night there, and the next morning Jeremy was summoned to see the C.O. to explain what happened. The mechanic who had serviced the plane said there was nothing wrong with it, inferring it was Jeremy to blame. However, the C.O. appreciated the fact that Jeremy could do nothing about it and dropped the matter. But it was not a happy start.

January 1944 was not a good month for the ship, or the squadron. They had spent the whole time on anti-submarine patrol in the Atlantic, and on their return to Greenrock they only had one serviceable Swordfish. The remaining eight had suffered damage, due mainly to bad weather, and one pilot error.

The following month was all Atlantic convoy duties. They would escort the convoys to within flying protection of the American coast, and then escort the convoys on the return journey. Landing on the flight deck at sea was always a tricky manoeuvre. During one such landing his pilot crashed onto the Barrier, and although there were no injuries, the plane was severely damaged. On another occasion they had landed very heavily, breaking the undercarriage. Once again luck was on their side as the two depth charges they were carrying were not primed to explode.

The time in the Atlantic was spent in company with Capt. Walker and his corvettes in hunting German U-boats.

During April and May most days and nights were spent in convoy protection which could take them as far as Gibraltar. One night the pilot made thirteen attempts to land back on the *Audacity*. "I thought my luck had run out," he recalls, but the next attempt was successful.

But Swordfish did go over the side. In one such incident when one did go over the side the pilot and navigator were rescued, but the TAG, who was a friend of Jeremy and a leading airman, died as a result of the flames from the flares being ignited. They buried him at sea the next day.

In October 1944 under the Lend-Lease programme the *Audacity* saw a drastic change in her mission and station. No longer detailed for the Atlantic run she was ordered to do convoy protection duties on the Murmansk run to Kola Inlet.

These convoys were huge and could have up to fifty merchant ships, and although this was the shortest and most direct route it was also the most dangerous. They ran from Iceland in the summer months, but after September moved south to either Loch Ewe or Oban. These convoys needed protection from the threat of the German U-Boats. The corvettes and other escort ships often experienced problems with their anti-submarine detection equipment due to the extreme water temperatures. Leningrad was under siege and in desperate need of supplies. These needs ran from aircraft, tanks, trains, ammunition, fuel and food.

This was a gruelling run, complicated by appalling weather conditions with temperatures well below zero most of the time. Snow and particularly ice were always present, and had to be constantly removed from the flight deck and arrester wires. Spray would freeze on contact and added considerable weight to ship and aircraft. In some instances on the smaller merchant ships it could cause the ship to capsize. The convoy could only maintain the speed of the slowest ship and as speed was absolutely essential this was a severe handicap for all convoys. The *Audacity* had no ice-breaking capability accept her size and weight. This applied to all the other ships in the convoys as well. Life on board was a constant round of shovelling snow over the side and chipping ice. Touching any metal object with bare hands caused the hand to stick to the surface, causing burns. Jeremy was to do three round trips to Kola Inlet.

The Russians showed their appreciation to all these seaman many years after the war when they awarded them a commemorative medal.

SEVEN

SWANLEY
NAUTICAL SCHOOL

Unable to care for my younger brother Glen and myself, Mother placed us in the Swanley Nautical School for Boys, in Hextable near Swanley in Kent. The home was intended to be for the orphans of naval officers, and although we were not orphans by any stretch of the imagination Joan pulled some strings and with the help, no doubt, of my father, had us accepted.

The home was situated on several acres, and was almost a self-contained community in itself. The headmaster, Mr. Collins, lived in a large two-storey house where we would gather occasionally for a sing-song whilst he played the accordion.

There were five other houses that were lived in, with twenty boys in each one. Two other houses had all the windows blown out, and the roofs caved in, having been bombed during the war.

Each house had a matron in charge, and a cook in the kitchen.

Downstairs was matron's private office, the dining room, kitchen and a games room, which was used for homework. To get from the dining room to the games room was a hallway with wooden tiles on the floor. This was always kept highly polished by the 'Bumper', a long handled thing with a heavy metal block on the end which we tied rags around. Complementing the Bumper, several boys would skate up and down the passageway with rags tied to their feet. The Bumper was also used in some cases as a form of punishment.

Upstairs was Matron's bedroom, two dormitories for the boys, and a single toilet. We were well looked after, scrubbed and polished, and what education we received, not surprisingly, was bent to all things nautical. Besides the Basic English and Maths, we learnt how to tie bowlines, reef knots, and sheep shanks. In the evenings we were taught naval history, seamanship, navigation, and the rules of the road, which was the equivalent of the Highway Code, but for ships at sea.

We wore a uniform of navy blue serge jacket with brass buttons down the front and three on each sleeve.

In the afternoons we played football. Two boys would be selected as captains and would pick their teams. One afternoon it would be battleships versus cruisers, another time it would be destroyers versus corvettes. Anyone watching from the touchlines would think it was a swarm of bees flying around. Once the ball was kicked twenty boys would run after it. Wherever the ball went it was chased by everyone. The goalie never had a chance.

The grounds were looked after by Mr. Uck whom all the boys considered to be ancient, but was only about fifty. Mr. Uck was ably assisted by a Clydesdale horse named Samson. Besides all the usual gardening, Uck and

Samson ploughed the field below the football pitch. We would see Samson pulling the plough making a single furrow, Mr Uck holding the reins urging him on .When the field was ploughed, potatoes were planted which no doubt were used by the home to feed the boys.

On Saturdays we received sixpence pocket money and were taken down the hill to the local sweet shop to buy sweets which were then handed over to the matron. Every night before going to bed we could pick one sweet from the bag. On Friday evenings we would be given whatever sweets were left in the bag.

On Sundays twelve of us marched down to the church, and donning cassocks and surpluses formed part of the choir. We always sang the naval hymn, 'Eternal Father strong to save'.

After several months at Swanley, Mrs. Crampton summoned Glen and myself to her office. With fear and trepidation we followed her, and after being seated she announced that we had a visitor. We spent a few anxious minutes fidgeting when in walked a tall, slender woman dressed in army uniform. I don't remember the conversation, but when she left she handed us a bag of sweets.

Afterwards we were told it was our mother. Up to that time we'd assumed that Mrs. Crampton was our mother.

꧁

One night when Mrs. Crampton was asleep, Glen, I and two other boys, Arthur and John, crept out of bed, down the stairs and we were away. We walked through the lanes and onto the streets and headed for London although none of us had any idea where London was. We were running away, not because of being badly treated, but for the sheer excitement of the adventure. We had no food and no money.

After walking for several hours we were beginning to tire, but as luck would have it we found a long wooden bench table with green felt tacked on the top. A notice nearby read 'Cider Apples for Sale'. We all took one and filled our pockets with the rest. One of the lads ripped the green felt off the table and we scrambled underneath and covered ourselves with the felt. Because the felt was not big enough to cover us all, arguments broke out. One boy would pull the felt this way; another boy would pull it the other. The table was at the end of the front garden of a house. Having been awakened by the noise, we made the occupant open his bedroom window and bellow, "What the fuck you bastards doing?"

We scrambled from under the table and took off running as fast as we could. Out of breath, we began walking again when it started to pour with rain. Looking for somewhere to shelter, we came across a red telephone box. Two boys sat on the floor, the other two stood, and although we could not close the door completely it was better than walking in the rain. We were huddled together in the telephone box waiting for the rain to stop when a police car drew up. They asked us what we were doing.

"We aren't pinching the money if that's what you think," said Arthur.

"Where are you lot from?" said the policeman.

"We're from London sir."

"London my arse, get in the car."

He drove us back to the home and rapped on the door. Dawn was just breaking.

Mrs. Crampton opened the door. Framed in the door she saw the policeman and the four of us standing there. The look on her face was total shock. She fell to the floor as if she had been poleaxed. The policeman rushed forward, kneeled beside her.

"Get a wet cloth," he shouted. We stood there rooted to the spot, and began to cry. We all thought she was dead. Needless to say we all did extra duty on the Bumper for a very long time.

EIGHT

THE PORT SIDE

Mother had been stationed in the Isle of Wight during the war, manning the anti-aircraft guns. She was also in Coventry placing dead bodies and body parts in cardboard coffins after Coventry had been heavily bombed by the German Air Force.

Whilst she was there she met Albert Plurien who was serving as a Wireless Operator in the Free French Navy .They had a son Paul who went to live in France with his Grandparents as they thought it would be better as Paul had TB.Alberts Father, a high ranking officer in the French Navy arranged for Paul to be smuggled aboard the French aircraft carrier the Arromaches (ex H.M.S.Colossus) which was anchored outside Portsmouth harbour in the Solent. Consequently Paul was smuggled aboard and taken to France to be brought up by Alberts parents.

It was a turbulent marriage from start to finish, but despite this a daughter Gabrielle was born. Albert for some reason never explained by Mother to the family was deported back to France.

Shortly after the war we had another visit from Mother at Swanley Nautical School. Matron led us into her office and made us sit down. She was there to ensure that we observed the strict code of ethics that had been instilled in us from the very first day at school. Please and Thank you being top of the list.We were not allowed to speak unless spoken to .We waited nervously in the office,after a little while Matron came in dressed in her thick tweed costume. The door opened and there stood Mother dressed in Army uniform, and said "Hallo Boys"

What both Glen and I remember about this visit was when Mother asked the question "Would you like a new Daddy?

Having not known a Father of any description and not knowing what they did, we were confused. Then Glen asked,

"What do Daddies do ?

Mother was a bit taken aback by this, but went on to explain how he would take care of us.

We would be leaving Swanley and going to a new home, where our new Daddy and her would look after us and everything will be so lovely, she said.

Our time at Swanley was now coming to an end. Mother came one day and collected us and took us to our new home . We arrived at a one bedroom flat in a converted mansion in Munstead Heath just outside Godalming in Surrey.

Our new Daddy came with two boys, two girls, a tent, and a bicyle.The tent was erected at the back of the mansion for the boys to sleep in, as there were now four of us.The girls slept in the flat with Mother and our new Dad.

Dad would set snares in the woods at the back of the property and catch rabbits, which Mother made into stew.

Mother then contacted the Housing authorities and it was arranged for us all to move to the new town of Crawley Sussex where we would live in a Council house. The girls were sent to their Grandparents in Fareham.

The natural assumption of most boys when they left the Nautical School was that they would join the Navy, and I never thought any different. For brother Glen it was not to be, as he entered a five year printing apprenticeship at Lloyds Register of Shipping in Manor Royal on the industrial site in Crawley.

Mother had been born to wealthy parents, which is partially illustrated by her education. She had attended St. Paul's College at Westminster in London, continued at the Sorbonne in Paris, and completed her education at a finishing school in Geneva .She was fully bi-lingual and spoke English and French fluently.

However at seventeen years of age she was diagnosed as being schizophrenic. This was a closely guarded family secret which only came to light when we were adults. This went a long way to understand to some degree her instability and inability to maintain any kind of enduring relationship throughout her life. Little is know of the period between her leaving school and her first marriage as her sister, fifteen years her junior had only very vague memories of her growing up.

In November 1931 she had, very much against her Father's wishes, married a Mr. Charles Foss, a builders clerk, at the Register Office in Brentford, Middlesex.

Joan's Father despite his disapproval bought the couple a house for a wedding present. In April 1933 a daughter was born, but fourteen months later the baby died of bronchial pneumonia. What effect this had on Mother is unknown, but surely must have been damaging to her emotional and mental well being.

Then inJuly 1938 I was born in Andover Hants, followed eleven months later by my brother Glen who was born in Glamorgan Wales.

Harry C.Gaffney is recorded as the Father in both instances. Mother used to joke that our births were probably instrumental in causing the war.

NINE

THE START OF A LONG JOURNEY

I was fourteen when my mother took me on the train to London to a Navy recruiting office. She was told to bring me back when I was fifteen. I was a small boy and very shy, weighing in at 6 stone and 6 pounds (90lbs). Most people on first sight would have put my age at about twelve.

When we arrived back home, Mother suggested it would be a good idea if I found a job so I would have some money to go in the Navy with. Why I would need money for this I didn't know.

I went to Compton the local butcher. The shop floor was covered in sawdust and patrolled by Henry, an overweight cat. Under the scrutiny of the head butcher I learnt how to wring a chicken's neck, and then pluck them whilst they were still warm, and in some cases still twitching. I would pluck about twenty of these unfortunates daily and stood ankle-deep in feathers by the end of the day. Thus after impressing the butcher with my chicken-plucking endeavours he considered I was ready for the next step up the ladder and introduced me to the fine art of sausage making.

What Henry missed, because he was slow of pace, went into the sausage grinder. The scraps were dropped into the top of the grinder with one hand and the handle on the side was turned by the other. As the handle was rotated the assortment of leftovers was cut and ground into small pieces and forced through a protruding metal spout, which had a long piece of pig's intestines pushed on to it like a large condom. The entrails oozed out, filling the condom. When a yard or so of this gruesome stuff was lying on the wooden block it had to be twisted into sausage-length pieces by twisting the whole thing and then cut.

When Mother found out that I could earn a few shillings more at a small company that made wooden garden sheds, I left the butchers and started work banging nails into planks of wooden frames which made up the floor of the sheds.

It was a lean and tight operation. There were no tea breaks as the boss's wife would bring cups of tea around twice a day which we had to drink whilst working. When the timber lorries came in with a delivery it was another of my jobs to help the driver unload. It was heavy work and I would arrive home totally exhausted. At the end of the week I was paid 2 pounds and 10 shillings. I gave Mother 2 pounds 5 shillings and the rest was mine.

Mother would buy a bottle of gin and a packet of Du Maurier cigarettes, one of which was usually hanging from her lower lip. Standing at the stove one evening stirring something in a pot which was to be our evening meal, an inch-long piece of fag ash dropped into the pot. Totally oblivious as to what had happened she continued to stir.

A few months later we once again sat in front of a naval recruiter who wore a dark navy blue suit with brass buttons, and a cluster of medal ribbons. I thought he was an admiral.

I was given a medical, and though the minimum height required was 5 feet it was found I was only 4 feet 11.

"Never mind," the admiral said, "you'll soon grow."

"How long do you want to be in the Navy for sonny?"

It was a question I had never contemplated.

"Oh about two or three years," I said.

"It's twelve years minimum and the time starts when you're eighteen." In my mind that was nearly fifteen.

Mother said, "That's alright then isn't Patrick."

"Yes," I mumbled.

"You will be sent a train ticket to Euston station where you will be met by a Petty Officer. Don't worry there will be plenty of other boys there so you won't miss them?"

Mother was warming towards the admiral by this time and was very friendly.

Bored by their adult conversation I looked out the window and in the distance I could see Nelson's Column. I wondered if he would have been proud of the fact that another boy had just joined the King's Navy to earn the King's shilling.

I signed some papers and it was all done. I was going to be in the Navy!

After we left the admiral, Mother took me to a Lyons Corner shop and ordered a sticky bun and a cup of tea.

"What a lovely man, I'm sure he will look after you," Mother said.

I wasn't so sure about that myself. After all, the fact of the matter was he was a salty Chief Petty officer nearing his pension time that had probably seen more sea time than Nelson, and never wanted to have anything more to do with convincing young boys that they should do the same.

As I've mentioned her so much, perhaps I should tell you a little about her.

Mother was partial about three things in her life, mainly gin, men, and wedding cake, strictly in that order. She was fully bilingual in both French and English, was most articulate, and could charm most people on first introductions. She was not particularly attractive-looking, having protruding 'English teeth' and smoke-grey eyes that looked at each other. Unfortunately, despite her wonderful education, she had no idea of how to live life on a daily basis.

Some months later after receiving the train ticket I found myself stepping off the train at Euston station. There I saw a gathering of about two hundred boys milling about in small groups.

They wore Teddy boy suits, winkle picker shoes, had pork chop sideburns down the sides of their faces, gold chains around their necks, and knuckleduster rings on their fingers. Fags hung from their lower lips.

They looked a rough and unruly bunch of lads, laughing and joking, pushing and shoving each other. I stood to the side, in my school uniform, conspicuous in my short trousers and striped school tie.

A Petty Officer gathered us all together, and before boarding the train to the east coast handed us a brown paper bag which contained two fish paste sandwiches and an apple. The train carriage soon filled up with smoke. The brown paper bags were tossed out the windows when it was discovered you could buy beer on the train. A convoy of buses awaited us at Ipswich station which took us from Ipswich to Shotley, located on the banks of the River Stour opposite to the ports of Felixstowe and Harwich.

Card given to each recruit on joining the navy.

TEN

TO THE BEAT OF
THE DRUM

When I first joined the Navy
My heart was full of glee
I'd done my best
And passed the test
To be a British sailor.

G anges in 1954 was the largest training establishment
of its kind in the world for the training of future
seamen of the Royal Navy. At any one time there were
2000 boys there. Tens of thousands of them passed
through this establishment; it broke some, but the vast
majority survived and became better for it.

The first four weeks of our Navy life began at the
Annex. The very first thing that happened was we were
lined up and a gentleman with a pair of electric clippers
came along and ran it all round our heads right to the
top. Then into the kit-issuing room where we were
given a kitbag. We piled all the kit inside. Included in
this kit was a housewife, a wooden type that spelt out
your name, a pair of boots, a tin of Cherry Blossom
boot polish, gas mask, working clothes, (no.8s) serge

suit, (no.3s) underwear, socks and three hats, two black and one white. Inside the black hats was a red and green silk lining, so as our instructors told us there was no excuse not to know your port from your starboard. The underwear was an off-white colour, but was, after a few washes, expected to be white.

After one week we were taken to the laundry house to do our washing. The laundry room had two rows of concrete basins. We stripped down and stood naked in front of the basins and washed our clothes with a large chunk of carbolic soap, called Pussers Hard. After each item was washed we took it to the instructor for inspection. We stood in front of him shivering, as much from the cold as from what to expect next.

"Cuffs," he shouted. We showed him the cuffs.

"Collar." "Front." "Back."

If all proved satisfactory we went back to our basins and washed the next item. If not, the instructor would give you a slap with a thin piece of wood which he always had handy in his right hand which he held behind his back.

The next item on the agenda was swimming. "It is essential you learn how to swim as none of you will ever get to sea if you can't swim." Taken to the swimming pool, we donned canvas white duck suits and were told to jump in. Even for boys who could swim it was hard going. The only stroke taught was the breaststroke, for endurance, and the ability to float on one's back was also required. It was explained to us that one could last for days in the sea if we mastered these two things.

I, and several other boys who could already swim,

were lucky as this ordeal ended right there. For the unfortunate few who could not swim, the agony was prolonged much longer and they had to attend 'backward' swimming classes until such time as they could.

After four weeks at the Annex we were transferred over to the main establishment.

I and forty other boys were placed in 42, Mess Collingwood Division, a two-storey brick building that overlooked the parade ground. Others would find themselves in different divisions such as Benbow, Drake, all named after famous admirals. Opposite our mess on the other side of the parade ground was Nelson Hall. To the left was the mast. An awe-inspiring sight to us boys. Some spoke of it in terms of fear, others in awe; I saw it as a challenge and knew inside me that one day I would climb it.

Unpacking our kit, we jammed it into our lockers and waited for our instructor. Most of these instructors were chief petty officers or petty officers, all very experienced sailors having served at sea in World War Two, and experienced the Navy under war conditions. They were tough, brutally honest, but fair. What they taught you would stay with you for the rest of your days.

Gunnery Instructor, Petty Officer Jones stepped into the mess a few days later and bellowed,

"Empty your lockers."

We piled our kit in a big heap on the mattress of our beds and waited for further instructions. The mattress was quite thin and filled with picked oakum. We were shown how to fold each piece of kit to the regulation size, and how to lay it out in the prescribed manner for future kit inspections. Then we were shown where to stamp each piece where it would not be seen prior to stitching our name on it. This is where the housewife came into play. Inside this cloth bag were needles and red silk thread. For the next few days we sewed and sewed until every item of clothing had our name neatly sewed on. Metal punches were used to stamp our name on our pusser's dirk Seaman's knife (which had to be worn at all times), and cap box. After a day of sewing, the lights were turned off at 9pm when we turned in.

Many a day was spent on the parade ground where we drilled with the Belgian 303 rifle used in the Second World War by naval landing parties. Weighing 9 pounds, we slung this rifle around our shoulders, marching up and down in a totally disorganised rabble.

It was a frustrating exercise for us and the instructor,

but like most things we eventually got the hang of it and became something resembling a marching unit.

The parade ground was akin to holy ground, and if one wanted to cross it you were required to do this at the double; walking was strictly forbidden.

At the end of our mess deck was the shower and washroom where we washed our clothes standing at long wooden tables.

After a few weeks I volunteered for the bugle band, so attended sessions where I was taught to play. However, after two weeks of joining the band I was going to Bury St. Edmunds where an agriculture show was being held. I was placed in the centre of the back row and told to go through the actions with the rest even though at that stage of the game I could not play a note.

The bugle band always led the parade at Sunday divisions. It was first past the saluting base with the drum major swinging the mace, sometimes throwing it high in the air. Inclement weather would see the Sunday parade moved into Nelson Hall where the reverberations of the band increased the decibel levels to great heights. It was always an uplifting experience and made the hairs stand up on my arms.

Pay days were held on the parade ground. Holding our cap in front of us, two half-crowns were placed on the top. After several weeks this was increased to three half-crowns. With this money one could buy a writing pad, envelopes, and a half-ounce of tobacco. The remainder of the money which we were not paid was deposited into a Post Office savings book.

Wednesday afternoons was a make-and-mend

day which allowed us to spend time doing what we pleased. This usually meant sewing our name on our kit, or writing letters home. One Wednesday I decided to climb the mast. I did not tell the other lads, just leaving the mess and walking to the base of the mast. As I climbed each rope rung I felt it give slightly under my weight. Up I went. fixing my eyes only on the next rung. Reaching the Devil's Elbow I leaned slightly backwards and reached for the next rung. Another few rungs and I was at a forty-five degree angle to the ground, perhaps now a hundred feet from the ground. Up past the Devil's Elbow I continued climbing until the last part of the mast where there was no rigging at all. Gripping the mast around both sides, I pulled myself up and with my gym shoes giving me extra lifting power I reached the button. I could see the lighting conductor and heaved myself up and sat on the button. To stand up was the scary part and slowly, as my knees were shaking a bit by now, I stood up and gripped the lightning conductor between my knees. I raised both arms to shoulder height and stood there looking over the Suffolk countryside.

Coming down was easier, and never looking down I reached the bottom and stood there contemplating what I had just done.

It was a defining moment, a deeply personal one; besides a sense of achievement, I knew with everything that I was, that there would never be anything that the Navy could throw at me which would bother me. I was ready, and in my mind I had become a sailor.

With two weeks left to go at Ganges we were

measured for our sea suits. These would become our No.1 dress for special occasions and going ashore. We had learnt how to tie a tiddley bow on our cap tallies with a silver three-penny piece in the middle of the bow, and cut the ends into swallow tails.

Our instructor took us for a farewell run into Ipswich and we descended into a local pub that sold scrumpy. This rough cider was cheap and potent. Debris from the apples settled to the bottom of the glass. We asked the instructor what it was and he told us, "Don't bother about that, it's only a few fishes that make it taste better." We tried flirting with the women in the pub. But they had seen baby sailors before and were having none of it. However, we had a jolly good time and at 11pm we piled back into the coach for a good night's sleep back at Ganges.

We were now measured for our sea suits which would become our No.1 suit. The trousers would have 32-inch bottoms. Each leg would be pressed with seven horizontal creases and folded concertina style and placed under our mattress to keep them crisp and sharp. Our jumpers would be skintight which your mate would help you pull over your head and down your body. Gold wire badges and cap tallies were issued. I sewed the gold star on my sleeve showing I was an advanced boy, and the gold bugle badge on the cuff. The star meant that you could read and write I suppose but was really of no consequence. However, we all thought that we were ready and surely we must be top of the pile.

The next day we mustered in Nelson Hall. We were to be told what ships we would be going to and where they were stationed.

A few names were called out.

"Right, you lot our going to H.M.S. *Dainty*, and will serve eighteen months in the Mediterranean."

More names called out.

"You lot are going to H.M.S. *Liverpool*, and will serve eighteen months on the West Indies Station."

A lot of the boys were excitedly talking by now and were not paying any attention to what the instructor said. The boys who had not had their names called out yet waited anxiously to hear their destiny.

"The rest of you will be going to H.M.S. *Maidstone* of the Home Fleet. She is moored in Portland Harbour."

"Moored." We were the laughing stock of the recruitment. The other boys were all going to seagoing ships in exotic places, and we would be stuck in wet and windy Portland. To say we were disappointed would have been an understatement. We had started Ganges as Boy Seaman 2nd Class, but were now going to sea as Boy Seaman 1st Class.

ELEVEN

MOTHER SHIP
MAIDSTONE

In March 1955, aged sixteen, I and twenty other boys stood on the jetty in Portland Harbour with our kitbag and hammock looking through the mist at a huge grey shape out in the harbour. Alongside her I could see the black shapes of submarines tied up. They were mainly submarines of the S-class and included *Seraph*, *Springer*, *Sea Devil*, and *Sidon*. There had been sixty-two of these 'S' built boats and they became the largest class of subs built for the Royal Navy. She could, at any one time, have as many as a dozen boats tied up alongside her.

It was true. She was moored, head and stern to two buoys. As the mother ship to the Second Submarine Squadron she had a huge responsibility in the operational wellbeing of the dozen or so 'S' class under her jurisdiction. She also to some extent had a moral and social responsibility to the submariners themselves.

By 1955, the *Maidstone* was old and tired and in an ideal world would have been given a thorough overall and refit. Launched in 1937 she had seen action in the Second World War, landing troops along the North

African coast. She had then moved on to Trincomalee in 1944, and sailed down under to Fremantle in 1945 via Subic Bay in the Philippines, and Hong Kong. In 1947 she had returned to the U.K.

She was a huge ship, with a high freeboard, but light for the size of ship she was. The artificers on board boasted they could make any spare part that a submarine may require. In her vast hanger-like light and heavy machine shops she was fitted with lathes, drilling machines, turning tools, welding torches, and tool boxes with every type of tool that was ever made. She carried a hundred torpedoes and mines in addition to diving and salvage equipment.

For such a big ship she was lightly armed but of course she did not go to sea on her own in times of war. She had four 4.5 mountings. One for'd on the forecastle just behind the breakwater, one aft on the quarterdeck, and two amidships. one on each side. In addition she had the lighter anti-aircraft guns consisting of four 4-barrelled pom poms, for some reason called Chicago Pianos. These guns had a high rate of fire but became overheated very easily despite having a water jacket around the breech mechanism which was there to keep the temperature down. Clips of ammunition were loaded from the top and dropped into the firing chamber. They made an ear-splitting crack when fired, far worse than the bigger guns.

She was a two-funnel ship; the forward one was, however, a dummy one.

She was also fitted with numerous Carley floats which in the event at a disaster at sea were thrown overboard to act as lifeboats. They were oval-shaped and made of cork, but by this time had been painted ship-side grey so many times that the ability to stay afloat for any length of time was questionable. Rope handles around the outside were there for the stranded who couldn't get aboard.

The boys' mess deck was as forward as one could go in the ship. The only thing more forward was the cable locker which housed the huge chain links of the anchor cables attached to the two 6-ton anchors. Welded to the other side of the cable locker bulkhead, 18 inches apart, were a row of hammock hooks. On the after bulkhead another row of hammock hooks. Therefore the depth of the mess deck was between 6 and 7 feet. The mess deck went from one side of the ship to the other. On each side there was one porthole. There were two wooden tables slotted into the deck and held by two pins. The pins had never been inserted in the correct position to hold the tables in place, but this did not become apparent until the day we went to sea. Lockers for our kit and personal possessions were stacked three high up against the for'd bulkhead. Twenty boys lived, ate, and slept here. We were a good bunch and got on really well. This was not surprising really as we were all in this together for better or for worse, but fortunately it wasn't until death do us part.

A boy's routine was established which was different from the rest of the ship's company. We got up in the morning before the rest of the ship's company and scrubbed the quarterdeck. Removing our shoes and socks we rolled up our trouser legs and lined up four abreast and scrubbed fore and aft whilst the instructor sprayed the saltwater hose around the deck. Others scrubbed the wooden grates covering the bollards and other fittings. On mornings when we did not do this, we were taken ashore in the motor cutter dressed in shorts and gym shoes to run to the top of Portland Hill. The instructor would stand at the bottom and ring the quartermaster based in H.M.S. *Osprey* at the top of the hill to check that everyone made it to the top.

Another duty we boys had was midshipman's hammock boy. The middies paid us one penny a day to sling their hammocks in the evenings, and to lash them up in the morning, then every two weeks we would scrub and change then

As I had been in the bugle band at Ganges I was made the ship's bugler.

I liked playing the bugle in Portland Harbour as the notes would bounce off the hills and echo around the harbour. Each morning I would go down to the quartermaster's compartment on the quarterdeck and play 'Reveille' to rouse the ship's company from their pits, then at 8am in company with the officer of the watch I would play colours on the forecastle where the Union Jack would be hoisted up the flag staff. Down at the quarterdeck the white ensign would be raised.

To get anywhere on the ship from the boys' mess we had to go through the for'd seamen's mess. You went up the ladder in the middle of their mess deck to the Well deck, or if you wanted to go further aft you had to walk the entire length and exit the door that led through to other mess decks and other parts of the ship. Each time we went into the seamen's mess we were greeted with "Green bastards, wait till you get to sea."

There were perhaps seventy to eighty seamen here, amongst them several hard cases who had served time in the Royal Naval Detention Quarters, but they were not all bad. They showed us how to lash our hammocks up in the right way. They advised us that one day if you found yourself in the water this could save your life. The tighter you lash it up, the longer it will keep you afloat. I hoped that day would never come.

One day, walking along the upper deck, I caught a glimpse of an Able seaman punch a Petty Officer, catching him flush on the jaw. The P.O. fell to the deck and the A/B casually walked away.

I did not know if this was an isolated incident or not. Nothing was heard on the mess deck, it was like it had never happened. It left me with an uneasy feeling, quite a disturbed one really. After all we had been trained at Ganges to stand to attention when addressing a Chief or Petty Officer and calling them Sir. I began to wonder if the Navy was such a good idea after all.

A buzz went round the ship that we would be going to sea. We would visit the port of Bordeaux and we lads became very excited about going to sea for the first time.

The day came, bright and sunny with a gentle breeze, when we slipped the two buoys, and with the assistance of a tug, the ship was manoeuvred through the narrow entrance of the harbour into the open sea. It was exhilarating. Here we were at sea with the wind blowing, the sea lapping against the ship's side. It was a wonder to me that a ship this size could push its way through the waves at all. I stood on the Well deck just looking down to the water line, amazed just to see the ship moving along. So this was what it was all about. I loved it. Yes, the sea was where I belonged, I knew that then. Everything had been worth it, and as the sea and the Navy were inseparable I was in the right place, just as I had known at Ganges after climbing the mast.

We sailed down the River Gironde and dropped anchor. We were to dock the next day starboard side to. The First Lt. decided he wanted that side of the ship painted, as we were showing quite a lot of rust. This was a big undertaking and the seamen did not take this news lightly. There was plenty of moaning and muttering, but nevertheless the starboard side was painted, and the next day we tied up alongside in Bordeaux.

Right opposite to the ship was a giant fun fair which gave away bottles of champagne as prizes. Liberty men could be seen returning from shore sides carrying bottles of champagne under each arm.

Back in Portland once again the First Lt. decided that the seaman should practise weighing the anchor by hand. This meant that the anchor would have to be connected up to the main cables and then dropped to the bottom of the harbour.

One of the seamen swung the mallet on the retaining shackle and the anchor plunged to the bottom. As there was no steam on the capstan the entire cable ran along the deck and piled up, alongside the anchor on the bottom.

Wooden spokes were inserted into slots on the main capstan and eight or nine seamen manning each spoke would start pushing the spokes around whilst trying to avoid any other fittings on the deck. Bearing in mind that the anchor weighed 6 tons it was really a back-breaking exercise. Round and round the seamen went, cursing, and swearing with each step. Link by link the cable latched into the lugs of the capstan. One seaman held the fire hose over the side and washed the mud and debris as it was slowly brought up from the bottom. Every so often a rest was ordered. So that the cable would not drop back to the bottom again, a huge safety catch type of fitting had to be secured onto the cable. All this was time and effort.

It took the better part of the day to get all the cable back into the cable locker and secure the anchor into the hawse pipe. It was another contributory factor in the events that were to follow. This was just another bone of contention between the seamen and the First Lt.

We were asked if we would like to go to sea in a submarine for a day. I did not go as life spent mostly underwater did not appeal to me, and it was not what I had joined the Navy for. However, several of the boys did go to sea on one of the subs. There was a mixed reaction from them when they returned, but one or two did express an interest. After all, submariners were paid (I think) 2 shillings a day extra.

TWELVE

MUTINY

R eturning from Bordeaux we took up our old berthing place out in the harbour in Portland. The Maidstone was never a happy ship during the time I spent aboard her. I was not to realise this at the time, and it was not until I served on other ships that I became to understand the difference. Morale was low on the seamen's mess deck. There was a core of troublemakers that appeared to run roughshod over the rest.

However, the ship now received sailing orders for Iceland to do fishery protection duties.

Assisted by tugs we went out the harbour entrance and steamed out into the North Atlantic, where after a few days of comparatively calm waters anchored in the bay in Reykjavik Harbour. For some reason only officers were allowed ashore to the town of Reykjavik, whilst all other ranks were landed on the other side of the harbour where the only distraction was walking, or hiking. There were few liberty men who chose this option. After a week's stay we went to sea. It appeared to the vast majority of the crew that we were going nowhere. It was just endless days at sea.

One day some genius came up with the idea of throwing a hand grenade over the side to see if they could catch some fish. I must say the result was indeed spectacular. The motor cutter was sent away to collect the massive amount of cod that had floated to the surface, stunned. There was enough fish to feed the entire ship's company of 700 for supper that evening.

Back to Portland Harbour, and settling into harbour routine. Runs ashore for the majority of the seamen were confined mainly to the scrumpy pubs where the rough cider was cheap and potent.

Tension between the seamen and the First Lt. was raised a notch by the First Lt. who allegedly called them "a bunch of cattle." The next morning when hands were required to muster on deck, the First Lt. found the Well deck covered in straw and hay, and the hands refusing to come up from down below to work. As we boys left the mess deck and went into the Forward Seamans mess to go to work we were told to sit on the benches in their mess. We were to become unwilling spectators to a situation which for us was hard to comprehend. Coming from the tight discipline and strict regime of Ganges this was sheer madness. However, we did what we were told to do and rather nervously sat down. A few minutes later the Masters at Arms came down to the mess deck and gave a chummy talk along the lines of "We know he's a bastard but let's get on with it."

He was shouted down and when he had left, the hatch at the top of the ladder was lowered. The only way into the mess deck now was through the door at the after end. Next came the Officer of the Watch who gave a lecture on the potential consequences they should expect if they did not turn to work. There was a sullen silence. Some of the younger seamen were very unsure of the situation, and given the choice, did not want to be involved, but felt intimidated by the ringleaders.

The forenoon dragged on. Some wrote letters, some played uckers (the naval version of the board game Ludo) and others played cards. The anxiety level was further increased when the Commander came over the tannoy, and ordered the hands to work.

This was met with ironic cheers, and the stalemate continued.

In mid-afternoon the Captain addressed the ship's company over the tannoy and informed them that he had been in touch with the Commander in Chief at Portsmouth and had briefed him of the situation. He further warned that:

"If the present situation continues, a detachment of Royal Marines will be sent for and the instigators will be arrested and removed from the ship."

One segment of the seamen who had not been willing participants from the start started to voice their concerns. They suggested that if the Marines became involved that they would place tear gas in the ventilation ducts which would force everyone out, so we might as well go up top and start work. The Ucker boards and cards had long disappeared by now. Arguments started, and the longer they went on, the nastier they became. There were threats and counter threats, but once again the ringleaders prevailed.

Late into the dog watches the standoff came to an end. One of the braver seamen stood up, and to the jeers and derision of the majority of the mess deck, walked out the mess and said he was going up on deck. He was followed by several others, and he told us boys to follow which we gladly did.

As we left, the Royal Marines and Master at Arms, lifted the hatch, came down into the mess, and escorted who they considered the instigators away in handcuffs. These men were court marshalled in Portsmouth, and it is believed they spent lengthy spells in the Naval Detention Quarters at Portsmouth, or in some cases dishonourably discharged from the Navy.

We never did see them again as they never returned on board.

꿎

The next day the *Maidstone* was ordered to sea. This time it was no jolly trip. We left Portland, turned to starboard and steamed into the North Atlantic up towards Iceland.

We were met by a stiff wind which cut the top of the waves off. Menacing waves as high as 20 feet hammered the ship head on.

Heading directly into the sea the bows of the *Maidstone* were lifted out of the water. As she came crashing down tons of displaced water shot up over the bows. Walking down the passageways you were lifted off your feet and for a split second one became weightless. When the ship came down and your feet touched the deck the weight of your body buckled the knees. After several hours it became quite tiring, but there were watches to keep.

Half-hour spells as lookout on the bridge, or telegraph man in the wheelhouse. As boys we would not be put on the wheel to steer the ship, but nevertheless we kept watch. In between times we sat in the flat just aft of the well deck. Feeling green about the gills, and hoping some fresh air would make me feel better, I went out on the well deck and, wedging myself between a wash deck locker and the bulkhead, sat down. Minutes later the contents of my stomach shot out of my mouth, and carried by the wind splattered on the bulkhead opposite. The next time I vomited it came right back into my face. I was miserable as sin, and wished I had never joined the Navy.

The *Maidstone* was rattling and shaking all over. We could hear crashing and banging all over the ship. Nothing had been properly secured or lashed down for going to sea as we had spent so much time in harbour.

Below decks was chaos. So this was what the seamen had been warning us about when they said, "Wait till we get to sea."

For some reason still unknown to this day only officers were allowed ashore into the town of Reykjavik. All other ranks who wished to go ashore were landed on the other side of the harbour, where walking, and hiking was the only attraction.

Morale was low, and this only served to lower it. After a few days we set sail for fishery protection duties. Ironically some genius came up with the idea of throwing a hand grenade over the side to see if they could catch some fish. I must say the result was indeed spectacular. The motor cutter was sent away to collect the massive amount of cod that had floated to the surface, stunned. There was enough fish to feed the entire ship's company of 700 for supper that evening.

Thankfully we steamed back to Portland in moderate seas, and once again secured to two buoys in the harbour.

Another thing us boys were always being asked as we passed through the seaman's mess deck was to have 'sippers' at tot time. Rum had been in the Royal Navy for well over 300 years, and had in some respects become the currency of the lower deck. The U.S. Navy had abolished rum way back in 1862, and the Canadian Navy was to follow suit much later in 1972. However, rum, in the 1950s. was very much part of navy life.

There was a strict code of ethics when drinking Nelson's blood at 110% proof. At the time of Trafalgar sailors were given double tots before going into battle. On the occasion of the monarchy's birthday when Splice the Mainbrace was ordered that also meant a double tot.

'Sippers' were given by everyone to the bosun who had fetched the rum and brought it down to the mess deck. 'Sippers' could also be earned by granting a mess mate a favour. A small loan of Blue Liners, so called because each cigarette had a blue line down the length of it, or tobacco which came in 1/2lb tins, each sailor had a monthly allowance of 300 blue liners, or a pound (LB.) of tobacco. The loan of some dhobey dust (washing powder) or a monetary loan of a few shillings to pay day.

'Gulpers' was stepping up, and required much more consideration. The loans were generally bigger. For half a tot, one would have to stay on board and do someone's duty watch whilst the other went ashore.

The Navy would pay 3 pence a pay to anyone who registered as 'T' or temperance. During my time in the Navy I only ever met one 'T' rating.

I had been on the *Maidstone* for fifteen months now and my time aboard her was coming to an end. The boys were given a form to fill in which was to determine which branch of the Seaman Division they would specialise in. There were three choices: Radar, torpedo and anti-submarine (TAS) or lastly Gunnery. I put my choices as listed here.

I was then informed my draft chit would be to the Gunnery Schol at Whale Island for a 3rd Class Gunnery course it set my career in a direction I did not choose, did not particularly like, but as I had been told many times before, "If you can't take a joke you shouldn't have joined the Navy." However my time on the Maidstone was not over.

THIRTEEN

TRAGEDY AT PORTLAND

In June 1955, I went for'd to play colours on the forecastle with the officer of the watch. I had just finished the call, the Union Jack had been hoisted and I was hanging around on the forecastle having a cigarette when there was a loud whoosh on the port side. I looked over the side to see three submarines tied up but one had just slipped its berthing lines and was moving around the bows of the *Maidstone* heading out to sea. The one next to it was in the process and she too moved to follow the one that had just left. The inboard one still secured to the *Maidstone* was the *Sidon*. She was due that day to go to sea for live torpedo firing. They were to test a new torpedo with a high test peroxide (HTP) motor. Naval scientists had picked up the idea from a captured German U-boat in 1945. Although HTP gave extra power to the motor, it was highly volatile.

We had become used to submariners on board. They were a hardy, happy bunch, and looked forward to coming on board. They could have a hot shower, a good meal, and a fitful night's sleep after returning from sea. One could always pick out a submariner apart from the ship's company, by their thick white submariner's jerseys and the smell of diesel that permeated their working clothes. They were held in high esteem by the ship's company and one could always see members of the crew taking their tots down to the submariners' mess deck for sippers, or gulpers.

I continued to look over the side. At first glance there did not appear as if anything unusual was going on. I then noticed the *Sidon*'s berthing wires had tightened up, and the *Maidstone* had taken on a slight list.

Sidon's berthing wires to the *Maidstone* had become so taut they snapped and the *Maidstone* gently came back to her normal upright position.

There were submariners in the water and some climbing up the gangway. The 3-ton crane operator lowered a wooden pallet over the side and a couple of submariners climbed onto it and were lifted inboard. Others simply slid into the water in a state of shock.

By this time it was apparent that something was drastically wrong.

The bow cap and rear door of the torpedo tube had been blown off the *Sidon* and she was taking on water that couldn't be stopped.

Surgeon Lt. Rhodes, a National Service Officer serving aboard the *Maidstone,* was the first man to board the *Sidon*. The electrical supply had gone and in total darkness, with thick smoke and toxic fumes, he entered the submarine. He brought one man out. He then went back down into the *Sidon* again this time with morphine and helped two more men out. Tragically he died in his third attempt at rescuing more men.

Sidon slowly sank to the bottom. Thirteen of the Navy's finest men died that day. All young men, some married with children.

An abyss of sorrow and sadness came over the whole ship's company.

A pall of gloom and despondency descended on the ship. Walking through the for'd seamen's mess deck was an eerie experience. None of the usual chatter and skylarking. No ucker games, or card playing. Mournful faces, staring with blank eyes. Some openly wept.

It was heartbreaking, eerie, and saddening for everyone on board. In our hammocks that evening we spent a sleepless night. We could hear the divers tapping the hull of the *Sidon* looking for signs of life as she laid thirty five feet below us on the bottom of Portland Harbour.

As a sixteen-year-old I could not really grasp the enormity of what had happened. We had always had a deep respect for submariners, for their daily courage of going to sea in these small, cramped, foul smelling craft. Any future ambition some of the boys may have had of being a submariner disappeared that day.

I wanted off the ship, but knew that was not possible.

A day later, I suspect the Admiralty wanted to avoid the media invasion that was expected; the *Maidstone* received sailing orders to proceed to sea.

༺ཉྩ༻

It was a raw, cold day, a stiff wind, and lashing rain when we ventured out of Portland Harbour As the cables were let go from the two buoys the wind caught the *Maidstone* broadside on which pushed her slowly but surely shore sides. Luckily by this time the cable had been connected up again to the 6-ton anchors, as the next order was to let go the starboard anchor. Realising we could not leave the harbour under our own steam, the captain requested the assistance of a tug. Once secured alongside, the anchor was raised and the tug attempted to turn the ship towards the harbour entrance. Unable to do so, a further tug was requested and between them manoeuvred the *Maidstone* seaward.

Once out of the harbour we turned to port and hit the open sea into a force six gale, and began rocking and rolling.

The boys' mess was in complete chaos. The portholes could not be tightened down as the threads on the bolts were rusted. The two mess deck tables had collapsed, and each time the ship plunged down more water came in. Lockers which had been stacked three high had come away from the bulkheads and all our kit, hammocks, plates, knives, forks, cups, and the remains of our last meal were sloshing about in a foot of water. The clips were fastened on the door, and the mess abandoned. The seaman in the forward mess deck thought all this was totally hilarious.

As we laboured up the Channel into the Bay of Biscay the severity of the storm was upgraded to force nine. The mountainous seas battered and bruised the *Maidstone* to the point where she began to flounder. She creaked and groaned under the tons of water that came crashing down on her. Water rushed along the decks with enough force to knock you off your feet. We could hear crashing and banging all over the ship as machinery and equipment came loose being thrown from side to side.

During the first watch that night I was detailed for two half hour lookout duties on the bridge. Up on the bridge I saw the radar antenna rotating which gave me a degree of confidence because I could not see anything through the binoculars. The mast head light swung in huge arcs across the blackened sky. After a few minutes my stomach came up to where my chest cavity was. The contents, picked up by the wind, were blown aft, and splattered all over the superstructure.

The storm raged all night and into the next day. During the morning watch I was detailed for the wheelhouse. We were now heading straight on to the heavy seas. The badgeman in the wheelhouse took one look at me, and said, "go and sit in the corner, you're no fecking use here."

Eventually we arrived at the mouth of the River Gironde and calm waters. The First Lt. ordered the port side of the ship to be painted as we would be berthing port side to. Large strips of paint lay hanging down the ship's side as it had not set properly from the recent painting in Portland.

A few hours later we sailed serenely, if I may use the term, up the Gironde and berthed in Bordeaux. Directly opposite where the ship berthed were a giant fun fair and the prizes awarded there were bottles of champagne. Needless to say a jolly time was had by all.

FOURTEEN

MOONLIGHT IN MOMBASA

On completion of the gunnery course at Whale Island, I received a draft chit to H.M.S *Comus* of the Eighth Destroyer Squadron stationed in the Far East.

There had been thirty-two of these ships built during the war, consisting of four flotillas having eight destroyers in each. The names of the ships in each flotilla began with either CA, CH, CR, or Co. The Cos were *Comus*, *Cossack*, *Consort*, *Cockade*, *Comet*, *Cockade*, *Contest*, and *Constance*.

Served Far East 1957-9 H.M.S.Cossack and H.M.S.Comus

Comus was a dream ship. Destroyers, known as greyhounds of the sea, were considered sailors' ships. The *Comus*, and later the *Cossack*, which we were to commission later on in the commission, were very special ships. Of the elite tribal class these destroyers were sleek, fast, had crisp lines and could slice through the green ones at 32 knots. They weighed only 1710 tons, but had a crew of 222. The crew were efficient and professional from the Captain down to the most junior seaman. The skipper commander, Wyke-Sneyd, in naval parlance, was a real 'Toff" and much respected by the whole ship's company. These destroyers were heavily armed, packing a big punch for a small ship. The crew worked like a well oiled machine. To have a year and a half in the Far East was what every matelot wanted. I was soon to find out why. By this time I was eighteen years old, no longer a boy seaman but an ordinary seaman drawing 25 shillings a week.

Cossack in heavy seas

The crew had mustered at Stanstead Airport and flown out to Entebbe in January 1957. We were billeted overnight at the side of the runway in tents we shared with black soldiers of a Kenyan Army Regiment. The next day we boarded a D.C. 3 aircraft and touched down in Mombasa. Stepping onto the tarmac we carried our kit bags and hammocks to a waiting lorry that took us to the harbour.

H.M.S. *Comus* lay alongside. The crew of H.M.S. *Modeste*, that had brought her here, had left the ship and were on their way home after completing their eighteen-month commission. This was the start of ours, and we were anxious to get on board, unpack our kit, and settle in to our mess decks.

It was hot and humid, and after a couple of days of settling in we were ready for our first run ashore in Mombasa on the east coast of Kenya. It had a cosmopolitan population, mainly Swahili and Mijikenda, the majority of whom were Muslims.

I had my first taste of Tiger beer. My run-ashore mate and I ventured into a male-only drinking establishment with very high ceilings. Wobbly fans swished the hot humid air languidly above our heads. The mosaic tiled floor was covered in peanut shells and crunched under foot as we made our way to the bar. With two ice-cold Tigers we found a table and sat down. After three or four Tigers one of the locals politely asked if he could join us. He was very friendly and spoke wonderful English. The conversation inevitably turned to women.

"I get for you a beautiful woman," he said.

Bearing in mind that I had no previous experience with the fairer sex, I was feeling quite excited, but at the same time, filled with fear and trepidation.

Stepping outside the bar, the three of us walked down a dirt alleyway boarded on both sides by straw huts. It was teeming with life. Men, women, and children squatted outside the huts in animated conversation. Dogs and chickens scurried up and down the alley and between the shacks. The stench from the raw sewage that ran down each side of the alleyway was quite overbearing.

The man with us had stopped, and was engaged in a rather animated conversation with a rather large black woman. Her florid pattern cotton dress clung to her sweaty, dripping body. Next to her stood a much younger and prettier girl, whom I assume was probably her daughter. Whilst the man was talking to this woman my mate and I stood to the side. After a while he came back to us and said for the pleasure of their company it would be two tubes of toothpaste, one bar of Palmolive soap, plus 2 shillings.

We handed them over to the man and my mate, taking the hand of the pretty young girl, entered a small shack beside us. My heart sank, standing their alone in the squalor and filth. The large woman then took my hand and led me into the shack next door.

Entering the dark dingy shack she peeled off her dress and laid down on a single steel cot with a thin, stained mattress. She looked like a baby beached whale glistening in the shadowy light. I started to undress, but did not know where to put my white tropical suit and underwear. Seeing a bucket in the corner, I tipped it up and emptied the putrid contents on the floor. I did not take off my shoes or socks.

Chickens were pecking around the earthen floor, stray dogs wandered in and out.

I now stood before her, completely naked, except for my shoes and socks. I could see the whites of her eyes, and two rows of shiny white teeth. By the look on her face, it looked as if she was smiling. I don't think she had seen a naked, skinny white kid before. I slid one of my legs over her large round stomach, but kept the other on the floor. After all there may be some traction required.

Then I felt something quite warm running down my anchor leg and realised one of the dogs had decided to relieve itself. I also became aware after a while that she had placed her hand between her legs, and have often wondered since whether I had made love to her hand or not. Maybe if I had been more knowledgeable at the time I could have got a refund. The most dreadful moment of this brief encounter must have been when I found a squashed dead fly under one of her gigantic boobs.

Totally confused by the whole business I dressed and waited outside in the squalor and filth of the alleyway waiting for my mate to exit the shack where he was dallying with the daughter. For some time after this I was of the opinion that sex was hugely overrated, and could not understand why so many hours at sea were spent talking about it.

Leaving Mombasa we steamed for seven days across the Indian Ocean arriving in the huge natural harbour of Trincomalee (present-day Sri Lanka) for a forty-eight hour refuelling stop. After taking on 600 tons of fuel and fresh provisions, we steamed for another seven days at sea after which saw us tying up alongside in Singapore.

FIFTEEN

SINGAPORE SLING

It was early January 1957 when the crew of H.M.S. *Comus* gathered at Stansted Airport ready for their flight to Entebbe. We had enjoyed Christmas and New Year at home and were now ready for our time on the China Station. The Navy had just changed overseas commissions from two-and-a-half years to eighteen months so this was a first. Also a first was that the Navy was to fly a whole ship's company overseas to commission a ship.

We boarded a much smaller plane, a Dakota DC3, to take us to Mombasa. The plane only carried about thirty passengers and we sat facing the back of the plane with our backs towards the pilot. At the rear of the plane were three wooden cases of Coca Cola and the stewardess told us if we wanted a drink only one of us should go at a time as it could affect the stability of the plane. The plane did not fly at any great height as we could see the pathways and roads below. However, we had a safe flight, although it was quite noisy. Landing at Mombasa we were taken by bus to the harbour and caught the first sight of the ship.

She was a sleek, fast-moving ship. Destroyers, known as the greyhounds of the sea, were what I had wanted to serve on since I had joined the Navy. They could slice through the ocean at 32 knots plus and go to sea in any weather. There were four other ships in the Eighth Destroyer Squadron: H.M.S. *Cossack*, H.M.S. *Cheviot*, H.M.S. *Concord*, and H.M.S. *Cockade*.

We were to go to sea as a squadron many times and execute squadron formation and manoeuvres. We would exercise with other Commonwealth navies and the American Pacific Fleet during this commission. The captain always saw this as an opportunity to show our American cousins what we could do.

Our kit bags and hammocks had arrived before us and were piled up on the jetty. We lugged them on board and stowed our kit in our lockers and the hammocks in the hammock storage area located in the mess deck just forward of the tiller flat where the emergency steering compartment was. Under our mess, separated by the ship's bottom plates were the twin screws which often shook the entire mess deck, especially when the ship ramped up the revolutions for high-speed manoeuvres.

The crew of the *Comus* consisted of fourteen officers, forty-four chief and petty officers, twenty-seven leading hands, and 107 ratings from all branches which included about a dozen boy seamen (baby sailors) going to sea for the first time. A small advance party had been flown out to Mombasa and were waiting for the rest of the ship's company to join them. Also, already on board were sixteen Chinese who would stay with us for the whole commission. The Chinese stewards who worked in the wardroom were classified as naval ratings and given rank accordingly.

Petty Officer Lam Chun Nam was in charge of the wardroom stewards. There were two leading stewards, Kwan Chip, and Tin Tak Fai. The ordinary stewards in the wardroom were Lam Fung, Cheung Kwong Kwok, and Mo Chun Keong. The wardroom galley staff was backed up by two Chinese chefs by the name of Siu Kit Wah, and Mar Ying Tong.

For the rest of the crew, Cheng Wong would assist the ship's cook in preparing meals for the ship's company. Back aft in charge of the laundry was Chu Yu Tse as dhobi No.1; dhobi No.2 was Lee Swee, ably assisted by two more dhobis, Lam Kit, and Mui Hwa Chih.

The dhobis ran the laundry, in good weather and bad. No matter what the weather or sea conditions they washed all our tropical uniforms and pressed them always to a high standard. We had Chung Shue Hing as No.1 sew-sew, and Chung Yen Sing as sew-sew No.2. They would repair our uniforms, sew on buttons, provide white tapes and do any mending job you requested.

Coming up the ladder from the after mess deck and just a few steps further aft was dhobis' domain. They would squat on the deck with their rice bowls and scoop their food down with chopsticks. They were gentle folk, extremely hard working, and very good sailors. They charged modest prices and preferably liked to be paid in Hong Kong dollars as most of them lived there. They would calculate the price of your washing by flicking the beads up and down the abacus.

Once the whole ship's company were aboard we left Mombasa and steamed for seven straight days across the Indian Ocean to the port of Trincomalee.

We had got to know our mess mates and some of the officers by this time. Our captain, Commander Wykes-Sneeyd, was an old salt and as a young midshipman had served on the cruiser H.M.S. *Norfolk* at the Battle of the River Plate. I was to write to him many years after I had left the Navy and he replied with a handwritten letter giving a brief history of his time at sea. During our commission he was a well liked and a respected skipper. He was a sailor's sailor, tough but fair, and always expected the best from the ship and his crew.

A Watch and Station Bill had been posted which told everyone on board what their duties were both at sea and in harbour. It told seamen which part of the ship they would work in harbour, the ship being divided into three parts. The forecastle, which members sarcastically reminded us was the sharp end. The iron deck which was amidships and the quarterdeck, known as the blunt end. Along with this information was the action station of every member of the crew.

The seamen manned the armament. For a small ship the *Comus* was heavily armed. Gunnery rates would man the three 4.5 heavy guns, and the two single 40mm Bofors.

Tordepo and anti-submarine ratings (TAS) would maintain and fire the quadruple 21-inch torpedoes located amidships. When launched over the side these torpedoes could run for 8000 yards at a speed of 40 knots. They also manned the two triple-barrel Squid mountings located aft. The ship would have to decrease speed before Squid were fired so as to prevent the Squid landing on the forecastle. When fired, the Squid bombs would fly up, and over the mast, and hopefully about a hundred yards in front of the ship. They would explode at a preset depth and made life for any underwater object quite terrifying. Ship's company not engaged in manning the armament were closed up in the magazines, and stationed at damage control points throughout the ship.

After refuelling and storing ship in Trincomalee we sailed for another seven days, down the western coast of Malaya before securing alongside at Singapore.

Shore leave was granted to the starboard watch and most, if not all, headed to the fleet canteen in the dockyard.

The canteen was very basic but functional. Ice-cold draught Tiger beer was sold by the jug, and overhead fans stirred the hot humid air above one's head. There was always someone playing the beaten up piano, and the floor was usually awash with Tiger beer. Finding a seat could be difficult but as everyone sat with everyone else you eventually found a seat and could swap yarns with guys from the other ships in the squadron.

It was jam-packed with matelots when we first visited and a riotous sing-song was in progress. The beaten up old piano with several pints of Tiger on the top, could be seen jumping up and down as the tunes were being belted out. On one of the tables next to the piano stood a three-badge seaman singing and performing the old-time favourite song of the old Navy,

'This old hat of mine has seen some stormy weather'. After the first stanza he would throw his hat into the crowded bar. As he sang each verse, another piece of kit would be removed and thrown into the crowded, smoke-filled canteen, until eventually he stood only in his shorts. In the last stanza, after removing his shorts and bending down, dozens of pints of ice-cold Tiger were thrown in his direction amidst much cheering and hilarity.

After a few pints of Tiger in the fleet canteen, you could either go to the Sembawang Bar just outside the dockyard gates, or catch a 'fast black' (taxi) to the small village of Nee Soon which was about the halfway point to Singapore itself.

In Nee Soon was the Happy Bar, the Oasis Café, a tattooist, and several shops. Failing that, one could go the other way, over the causeway to Johore Bahru in the Federation of Malaya. To go into Singapore itself meant a seventeen-mile trip in a fast black, so we would only go if there was a bunch of us to share the fare of the taxi.

The only road into Singapore was a two-lane, rough-surface tarmac job. There were few cars, but plenty of bicycles, usually loaded up with baskets on a carrier at the back. It was not unusual to see live chickens or other fowl in the baskets.

One night after a few Tigers in the dockyard canteen, my mate Topsy beckoned me outside. When I got there he was standing beside a 15 cwt. RN lorry and said, "Get in."

Stupidly I climbed into the passenger seat and Topsy drove off heading for the dockyard gates. Slowing down as he approached the gate, the policeman opened the gates and stepped out to check the lorry. At that instant Topsy stepped on the accelerator and sped through the gate. Arriving at Nee Soon, a barrier pole had been placed across the road and several policemen awaited our arrival. Topsy slowed down the lorry, and just before he reached the pole once again slammed down on the accelerator, smashing through the pole and sending the police in all directions. We sped on towards Singapore, but this time we had company. One of the policemen had jumped onto the truck and with his truncheon broke the window at the back of the cab. I grabbed the truncheon and wrenched it from his grasp and threw it out the window.

A police car with sirens wailing was following us but could not overtake as there was too much bicycle traffic coming the other way. Reaching Singapore it became decidedly more precarious as we were weaving in and out of traffic, and going through red lights, stopping at nothing.

We were passing a cinema that had a queue of people waiting outside when the police car rammed us into the cinema wall, scattering the waiting queue. The lorry came to a shuddering halt and the police pulled Topsy out and handcuffed him. They also dragged me out and did the same. We were placed in the cells at the local police station and left there until the next morning.

A turbaned Indian lawyer came to our cell and told the warden in no uncertain terms to take the handcuffs off and take us to a bathroom to wash and scrub up, as we were to appear in court that morning.

The court was packed with locals on various drug charges. Topsy and I were first up, and the cop who had jumped on the back of the lorry in Nee Soon was the witness for the prosecution. He said the chase had proceeded at seventy miles an hour, which was doubtful as I don't think the lorry could have reached that speed even with an expert driver at the wheel.

The divisional officer, who must have emptied the ship's safe, appeared and duly paid the fine. There is no doubt that we had received preferential treatment, for whatever reason, but we were grateful for it.

I personally felt very remorseful about the whole escapade as I felt, quite sincerely, that I had not only let the skipper down, but also the ship and all my mates.

Shortly afterwards, I went before the skipper as a defaulter for among other things, disgracing the Queen's uniform. We received punishment of extra duties and stoppage of leave. I had learnt a valuable lesson and for the rest of the commission kept a clean sheet.

We went to sea often from Singapore, mainly exercising with other ships of the squadron, but in March after only three months aboard her the Admiralty had decided to retire her. She had been on the China Station for ten years by then and would be taken home by the ship's company of the frigate, H.M.S. *Modeste*. She would then be towed to the shipbreakers yard for scrapping.

The crew of the *Comus* would now be billeted in the naval shore base in H.M.S. *Terror* at Singapore.

At this time one of her sister ships H.M.S. *Cossack* was in dry dock at Singapore just finishing a refit. The powers that be had decided that we should now take over her to become its new ship's company.

The previous *Cossack*, which was the fifth ship in the Navy to be so named, had taken part in the first and second battles of Narvik. She had been involved in the rescue of 300 British merchant seamen held aboard the German supply ship *Altmark*. Sadly at 2330 on the 23rd October 1941 she was hit by a torpedo from the German U-boat U563 on the port side between 'A' and 'B' magazines causing the for'd part of the ship to explode. Captain Berthon and 158 officers and men were killed. Fires broke out and abandoned ship was ordered. *Cossack* remained afloat; however, the weather worsened and the operation was abandoned. She finally sank on 27th. October 1941 about one hundred miles west of Cape Spartel.

The final hours of the fifth Cossack

Capt. Berthon was from Esher in Surrey and when the news of the sinking of the *Cossack* reached the people there the town started a fund to raise enough money to build another destroyer. The £1,000,000 required was reached and surpassed for a final total amount of £1.5 million. The extra half-million was used to construct a submarine.

This new *Cossack* had been in the Far East since 1945, and during the Korean War she had done long patrols up and down the Korean coast bombarding north of the 38th parallel.

The sixth *Cossack* (D57) built was almost identical to the previous one built and this was the ship we were about to commission.

SIXTEEN

SHOWING OUR PACES

After taking over *Cossack* she was ordered to Korea to cover the withdrawal of British, Commonwealth, and American troops. The war had been over for some time now. We had arrived at the port of Inchon early in

Cossack at speed.

the morning to see the P. and O. liner *Canberra* there to embark the troops. Looking shore sides one could see a column of soldiers four abreast stretching over the plateau and winding far into the snow-capped hills. It was an astounding sight. Thousands upon thousands of soldiers with their backpacks and weapons marching towards the beach. A sign at the port read: Through these portals pass the finest fighting soldiers in the world, the U.S. Marines. All day the troops kept coming towards the harbour.

That evening the Americans picked up our liberty men and drove us into the Eighth Army Camp base for an evening of entertainment and fun. On the way we saw the local currency strewn amongst the ruins which was once habitable buildings. Beggars stood amongst the rubble. They did not pick up the money, knowing full well it was worthless. Naked children scrabbled among the ruins looking for any remnants that may give them comfort. It was a human tragedy, the likes of which we had never seen before. A tragedy that gave us some understanding of what war was about.

Entering the base was entering a surreal world. A modern community with PX stores, barbershop, laundry, movie house, and night club. American script dollars was the one and only money that was viable and could purchase any goods. It was Little America, transplanted to the Orient, just south of a hostile warzone. As in most wars civilian casualties far outnumbered the military. Not that this was anyone in particular's fault; it was the nature of war itself. We were shown into the night club, and were made very welcome. A live band provided music for dancing. It was difficult to take in the contrast of what we had just seen on our way here, and what we were now seeing and hearing. Although the Americans had arranged this evening for us as a "Thank you" it was a bittersweet experience.

We left Inchon a few days later, as did thousands of others, leaving behind a devastated land where misery and sadness was the legacy preserved in the memory. Leaving Inchon, the ship sailed south through the Korean straits to Pusan. After a brief refuelling stop there, we proceeded to sea once again where we were to do live shoots of the main armament. A plane, trailing a 1000-foot wire with a red silk chute attached, was our target. The gun training we had at H.M.S. *Excellent* was now put into practice. Teamwork, and split-second timing when firing 4.5 guns was essential. The window of opportunity was measured in seconds when a ship was attacked by an aircraft flying from left to right, or right to left. The use of ear plugs was not permitted as it was considered that no orders would be heard over the noise of the cordite explosions. Instead we were told to keep our mouth open during firing to allow the sound to pass through the ears, and out of the mouth unrestricted. The crack of the gun still tended to rattle your head on its way through. It also meant you inhaled a lot of smoke from the burning cordite that sent the shell projectile on its way to the target. There was always the outside possibility that whilst the radar was tracking the target, which directed the guns, that it would run along the towing wire and the plane could be hit.

The order to open fire was given and we saw the first shot explode slightly behind the chute. However, the next round hit the chute right where it joined the towing wire, and we saw the chute come floating down into the sea. There was much jubilation, and the skipper ordered the sea boat away to recover it. No.1 sew-sew would make an emblem of the ships crest on the two nacelle covers for the director situated high up on the bridge of the ship which we proudly wore for the rest of the commission.

We arrived in the southern Japanese island of Sasebo a few days later in company with the *Cockade* and *Cheviot*. The local newspaper reported our arrival, roughly translated as the following: Three British destroyers *Bebit* (1700 tons), Commanding Officer – Captain C.W. Marison. *Casac* (1700 tons), Commanding Officer – T.L. Copp. *Cockward* (1700 tons), Commanding Officer R.E.S. Wicas, will enter Sasebo on 7th August. Meantime the ships will be refurnished and members of the ship will take 'rest'.

There was not much rest. Ashore, in every bar, beautiful, petite Japanese women were very friendly and accommodating. After my first sexual encounter in Mombasa I was anxious to see if the experience could be improved upon. Entering an immaculately clean room the young lady insisted I have a shower. I stood under the shower whilst she washed me down with a huge soapy sponge. Only then would she lie down beside me. I must say with all modesty, I thought I had died and gone to heaven. So this was what it was all about. I had a better understanding of how wonderful a woman's company could be. I formed the opinion then and ever after, that women were God's special creation, to be loved and cherished. I have never lost that conviction, discovered in the arms of these Japanese beauties.

We were to visit the ports of Beppu, Yokosuko, Kobe, and Nagoya. As we tied up alongside, many of the girls from Sasebo were on the jetty waving the ship in. Whilst in Yokosuka we tied up alongside an American destroyer. After meeting some of their ship's company ashore the previous night we invited them on board the following day at noon hour to share some rum with us. Two young American sailors, one from Texas called Buddy, and the other from Georgia, duly arrived in the for'd mess deck and were given 'sippers' of rum all round and a generous helping of the 'Queen's'. The one from Georgia named Leroy, now slightly bleary-eyed, looked round the smoke-filled, crowded mess deck at the sweaty, tattooed bodies. There were a couple of off watchmen asleep in their hammocks overhead, and he said, "Gee you guys live like goddam pirates." We thought this was highly amusing. They in turn invited us on board. We sat in the air-conditioned mess deck whilst our hosts gave us Coca Cola, dispensed from a vending machine attached to the bulkhead, and as much ice cream as we could eat. This also came from another vending machine.

For a teenage lad, I didn't think life could be any better. We spent a total of five weeks in Japan, but all good things come to an end, and leaving behind the land of the rising sun, we sailed for Hong Kong back to our old haunts in Wanchia.

We returned to sea for more exercises and joined up with units of the American Pacific fleet. On a moonless night, the *Cossack* following astern of the midway class carrier U.S.S. *Shangri-La*, we watched as the planes circled overhead, waiting for their turn to land on the flat top. As the F2H banshees approached we saw them come down, dropping there tail hooks to catch the arresting wire which would bring them to a halt. Once stationary, the flight deck crew pushed them to the side in readiness for the next arrival. The *Shangri-La* and the *Cossack* steaming on the starboard quarter were doing 20 knots steaming directly into the wind.

The next Banshee, throttling down, came at the *Shangri-La* at an odd angle. It missed the arresting wire, and the pilot, slamming on his wheel brakes, sent the Banshee spinning in crazy circles along the flight deck before plunging into the sea off the port side of the bows. *Cossack* immediately turned to port, switched on the search light and scanned the area, but there was no sign of the plane or the pilot. The whole incident had taken only a few seconds, but one plane and one pilot had been lost forever to the unforgiving seas. *Cossack* took up its station again, and mercifully the remainder of the squadron all landed safely.

At daybreak we parted company from the *Shangri-La*, and set course for the west coast of Malaya to further assist the Army in their fight against the Communist Terrorists. We were to bombard the jungle hideouts of the CTs. A small army spotter plane circled high above the jungle. As each broadside was fired the observer in the plane would inform the ship where the shells had landed so our gunnery officer could relay the information to the transmitting station below decks. In the transmitting station men stood around a large manual computer apparatus where such information as wind speed, ship speed, range of target could be fed into the transmitting table which in turn trained and elevated the guns. After each broadside we waited for the corrections to be made, then fired another broadside. Down below these broadsides would sometimes blow all the lights, and the asbestos insulation would drop from the deck head. For us it was all in a day's work.

I cannot imagine being on the receiving end of these broadsides. The CTs must have been caught completely unawares, and to have this load of explosives dropped into their midst must surely have been instant death. There hideouts must have been completely obliterated.

SEVENTEEN

A FEW HONG
KONG DOLLARS

After leaving the *Comus* the crew were billeted in
H.M.S. *Terror*, the shore base in Singapore. It was
a treat to sleep in a stable bed and to be able to walk
around without getting wet or holding on to something.

The previous ship to bear the name *Cossack* had been involved with the rescue of 300 British seamen held captive aboard the German supply ship *Altmark* in Josing Fjiord, Norway in February 1940. In our trophy case on board the present *Cossack*, the sixth ship to carry the name, we had a silver tray presented to the ship by the seaman who had been rescued. Tragically, a little time later, off the coast of Gibraltar she had been torpedoed. The complete front end of the ship from the bridge for'd had been blown off with the loss of 144 lives including fourteen boy seamen. She was taken in tow, but after two days she sunk.

During the war she had been adopted by the national newspaper the *Daily Mirror* and was forever after known as the *Daily Mirror* ship.

Whilst the ship's company was in H.M.S. *Terror* the captain thought that this would be an opportunity to give the ship's company some leave, and some of the crew did indeed fly home.

However, the Army at that time was engaged in fighting communist terrorists that had infiltrated Malaya from the north. They roamed the jungle in small groups. Leaving their jungle hideouts, they cut communication lines, set fire to the rubber plantation estates, booby trapped roads known to be used by the locals. The big target for them was undoubtedly the railway. They were known to blow up railway bridges, and even the trains. They were a dangerous and elusive enemy and the Army would wage war with them for ten long years.

The captain again called for volunteers to go up country to assist the Army.

Quite a few of the lads did go, but I did not. They were fully equipped and armed, and boarded a train to Kuala Lumpur. After another train trip further up country,they were greeted by the C.O. of the Rifle Brigade. Here our lads were divided into three groups, and further equipped, this time with Army kit. They travelled by train up country and then were then driven to separate camps and for the next ten days they were under canvas.

There were three main villages in this part of the country, each ring-fenced as were the rubber plantations.

Workers were checked going in and coming out. Their identity cards were scrutinised, and the food they brought in for their daily meals was also checked over. Communist terrorists (CTs) were able to contact these workers, and were always on the lookout for new recruits to their cause. Some of our lads ventured into the jungle with the Army patrols.

These patrols usually lasted five days and nights, and for the lads from the *Comus* it must have been a harrowing experience. They walked in single file led by an Eban tracker, who, armed only with a machete, would lead then through the dense undergrowth of the hot, humid jungle. They could maybe penetrate 2000 yards in a day before laying up for the night. A piece of cord was tied around the ankle of each member of the patrol as they slept. A tug of the cord would alert them to any unwelcomed presence. The biggest fear was of ambush. Not knowing where or when they would be led unintentionally into a waiting group of CTs.

A lot of the soldiers sent to the Malayan jungle were serving their compulsory National Service of two years duration. They must have thought they had drawn the short straw getting this assignment, as many others never left the shores of Britain. Not that this was any fun for the lads of the *Cossack* either, but they all came through it and afterwards could say it was a worthwhile adventure.

Our time in *Terror* was like a holiday. We swam in the pool, and drank cold Tiger beer in the evenings. Some nights we went to Sembewang, a small village about halfway to Singapore. It had one main drag with bamboo shacks on each side. Some of these shacks were bars, but at the end of the street was Johnny Gurkha's tattoo abode. I was one of his customers, and by the time we took over the *Cossack* I had both arms and forearms covered with Johnny Gurkha's artistry.

Our time in *Terror* was coming to an end. The *Cossack* refit in Singapore Dockyard was now completed. We would shortly be going on board and settling in the same mess decks as we had on the *Comus*.

There would be no need to change the Watch and Station Bill as the only difference between the *Comus* and the *Cossack* was the name on the ship's bell, and the pennant numbers painted on the ship's side. We took our kit on board, stuffed our kit into our lockers and stowed our hammocks in the hammock netting. We had little time to get really organised as the following day we slipped our berth and steamed north into the Pacific, heading for Hong Kong.

It was a smooth passage with no adverse weather to contend with. The sea was generally calm and the skies bright. Flying fish followed alongside the ship in groups of about a dozen. They would leap out the water, spread their translucent wings flying over the surface of the sea for a few feet, then dive back again under the water. Porpoises in small pods, up near the bows, rubbed their bellies against the ship's side.

After several days at sea we approached Hong Kong Harbour, also known as Ha Wan. We lined up on deck in our tropical whites, saluting other ships as we entered. It was crowded with units of the American Pacific Fleet, merchant freighters, junks, and sampans. Secured alongside, we reverted to harbour routine. All-night leave was granted to the ship's company with leave expiring at 7am.

Hong Kong in 1957 had two huge dry docks for ships needing a bottom scrape or other repairs. Later in the commission the *Cossack* would be in one of them for just that purpose.

The first stop on a run ashore was invariably the China Fleet Club where we celebrated Christmas Day. The booze was cheap, and English brands of beer could be bought. The more adventurous would board the tram and venture into Wanchai. The tallest building on the island at that time was the eight-storeys Luk Kwok Hotel. The base of the Peak was dominated by shacks made of bamboo poles, corrugated iron, sacking, and flattened cardboard boxes on the floor. There were some one- or two-storey brick buildings where families lived, but families living in the shacks had to go to a communal water tap with bowls and jugs to get drinkable water.

Wanchia was a teeming mass of human bodies. 2000 Chinese people packed to the acre, at the base of the Peak. It was said at the time that the higher up the

Peak one lived, the more affluent one was. The streets were packed with every conceivable hawker. Every few steps was a girlie bar, or opium den. Tailor shops which could make a custom-made dress in a myriad of fabrics from silks to cotton. Men's suits, evening jackets and sportswear. Custom-made shoes, from brogues to casuals in many different leather colours ordered and delivered all in twenty-four hours. Tattoo shops with red and blue neon signs bent into Chinese characters, or English letters. Brothels, where olive-skinned, smiling Chinese and Philippines girls welcomed you in.

Men and women dressed in cotton pyjama suits, wide-brimmed straw conical hats, and flip flops. Open-fronted shops, and stalls. The clatter of mah-jong pieces as groups of men moved the ivory tablets around the table top. The smell of outdoor cooking wafting in the air, cooked on coal-fired braziers. Bean sprouts, fish, prawns, crabs, and rice all mixed in together.

Chinese men squatting on the pavement could sell you anything and everything from colourful macaws to smaller song birds in little wire cages. Rolex watches, watches with the finest Swiss movements, French perfume, Dunhill cigarette lighters, and pipes, paper ornaments made for the next life, bracelets, rings, necklaces, diamond ear rings in gold and silver all expertly handmade.

Rickshaws were the preferred mode of transport for most of the locals, but there was a tram system. Sitting opposite me on the tram one day were an elderly Chinese couple. The man was suckling on the drooping breast of the elderly Chinese woman. Nobody on the tram was the least bit concerned at this but it did stir my curiosity. The next day, on board, I asked dhobi No.1 what this was about. He told me that the man was probably a heroin addict, and this was some kind of Chinese therapeutic remedy.

The girls who worked in the bars were chosen for their good looks and their ability to speak English. Sitting down at a table she would take the order which included one for her. Her drink, which was non-alcoholic, would be served in a cocktail glass with a cocktail stick stuck into a cherry. She would be given a plastic chip by the bar owner for each drink. At the end of the evening the chips would be converted into cash. She would sit with you for as long as you stayed in the bar. She was attentive, polite and gracious. She would mop your brow if you were sweating, light your cigarette when needed, go to the bar whenever you wanted another drink. This is how I met Ah Kum, a beautiful, petite Chinese bar girl. Her name translated to English meant, Good as Gold. I took to calling her Goldie. She wore an embroidered cotton pyjama suit and a ponytail when she was not working in the bar, but on special occasions she wore the more traditional silk cheongsam with a slit up the side of her leg. All 5 foot tall, her skin was smooth as silk. She had a small, rounded face, with dark almond eyes, and pert, little pear-shaped breasts, and a smile that drew you in, and said welcome.

Ah Kum took me to her humble abode, at the base of the Peak that evening. It was a shack divided by a curtain where her mumma san slept on one side of the curtain and Ah Kum and I on the other. Mumma san had grey wispy hair and few teeth, two of which were gold. They cooked on a small primus-like stove. Into the wok went fried rice, meat, prawns, and bean sprouts. Water was fetched from a communal tap and carried back to the shack in a chipped enamel bowl. The price for a bowl of water was 10 cents.

I fell asleep that night in the arms of Ah Kum. In the morning I found my tropical uniform had been washed and pressed and neatly folded at the foot of the cot where Ah Kum and I had slept. I left a few Hong Kong dollars under mumma san's pillow and wended my way down through the shacks and caught a rickshaw back to the ship.

It became routine for me to see Ah Kum each time the ship returned to Hong Kong. We would go to the cinema watching Chinese films with English subtitles, or English films with Chinese subtitles. She bought me a pair of civilian trousers and a shirt as she did not want me to wear my uniform.

These kinds of liaisons were not encouraged by the higher authorities. Indeed permission to marry could only be granted by the captain. One such request by a mate of mine resulted in him being put on the first flight out of Kowloon and flown back to the U.K.

The *Cossack* now sailed back into the vast expanse of the Pacific Ocean to go down under for a visit to Australia.

We called into Suva. The Fijian police band stood on the jetty and played us in. Ashore we went through the swing doors of the only hotel bar in town and drank beer. Other times we sat on the lawns in a circle with the locals drinking kava out of coconut shells. We sang songs and clapped our hands. The locals were friendly, courteous, and spoke wonderful English. We were to visit Suva again later in the commission, and receive the same welcome. It left an indelible impression on one, one that left you in no doubt that all human beings are basically friendly, and desire the same things. Just like when we entered harbour, they bade us farewell in the same manner.

We now sailed to go down under. The first port of call being Fremantle on the east coast. But we had to get there first.

We were met by Typhoon Wendy which, on the Beaufort Wind Force scale, was approaching force nine, and try as we might to steer clear of it she followed us. Reading about the Beaufort scale meant nothing now.

It did not prepare you for what the real thing was. For two days and nights we stayed on the outer fringes of the eye of the storm. We knew of it coming and lifelines had been rigged down each side of the ship, but now they were redundant. If you were caught out on the upper deck you would surely have been swept over the side. If that had happened in these seas you were gone forever.

The captain made the only decision a good skipper would make in these circumstances. He turned the ship directly into the seas, meeting it head on. Alternatively, putting the ship broadside onto the seas, where the giant waves would hit the ship amidships, could put the ship in the position of capsizing.

Mountainous seas came at the ship, lifting the bows out of the water. On the bridge the forecastle came up and looked you in the face. At the after end the screws dug deep down into the angry sea. Just when you thought the ship would come down it was hit by another monster wave. The bows hung in the air a few moments longer. The quarterdeck was totally awash. Then she came crashing down with a mighty thud. Tons of water came up and over on to the open bridge, drenching the skipper and lookouts. Water sloshed around the bridge, draining down onto the signal deck and down the ladder to the wardroom flat where the officers lived. Smoke streamed from the funnel in a horizontal strip, disappearing as soon as the wind caught it.

Severe winds, bent halyards and radio aerials back in long curves. It swept down the whole length of the ship.

It flattened your face, and the eerie piercing sound of the wind whistled past your ears. Spray whipped into the face, stinging the eyes, rivulets of water running down the back of the neck. Yes, I thought, this is the Navy; this is what I joined for. We've got a real ship here, and real sailors. It was the most frightening but exhilarating experience one could ever imagine.

But we had faith. Not the religious kind, but faith in the captain, and the ship. We had faith in the welders, the rivet men, the fitters, and the hundreds of ship workers, both men and women who had worked in wartime Britain to put it all together.

At the same time as the bows dug into the seas, the back end lifted clear of the water, the screws turning frantically with nothing to bite into, shuddering the whole frame of the ship.

All hands had to remain at whatever station they were at when the storm had broken. No one was allowed on the upper deck and the chef in the galley was reduced to making Kai. He made this by shaving slivers off a large slab of chocolate into a metal pot and adding boiling water. The resultant drink and hard tack biscuits would sustain us for the next two days.

In the wheelhouse one of the boy telegraph men had brought his dhobi bucket with him. Green bile now slopped from side to side. The gyro tape sped from one end of the illuminated strip to the other. A putrid smell pervaded the small enclosed space. The face of the coxswain on the wheel, an old wartime veteran, was drawn and haggard.

Moving from one place to the other below decks was almost as hazardous. Walking down the main passageway one had to stretch out your arms to avoid bouncing off the bulkheads. For the baby sailors on board it proved to be a harrowing experience; one of them suffered a broken arm after being thrown against the bulkhead.

Down below in the engine and boiler rooms, stokers watching the gauges saw the needles erratically swinging from one extreme position to another. Drenched in sweat their overalls clung to their bodies.

Off watch men sleeping in their hammocks had no sleep either. As the front end of the ship was thrown up there was a feeling of weightlessness, but as she came down, the total weight of the upper part of the body could be felt, which, if you were dozing off, would bring you around with a jolt.

The seas kept coming at us, bodily lifting the ship out of the water. Occasionally a rogue wave would catch the ship when the front end was up in the air, and knock the ship sideways. We were making very little headway.

Gradually the storm abated. The winds eased, and the seas became less angry. And on the second day the sun came out. We undid the deadlights on the portholes, and put the wind scoops out. Fresh air blew through the mess decks. The crew came back on the upper deck and lounged around, sitting on the deck leaning on the bulkheads having a smoke. The sun had dried out the upper works, leaving a film of thin salt behind.

We steamed now in calmer waters approaching the western coast of Australia, and the port of Fremantle. We washed down the paintwork, tightened up the stays and guard rails. Signal men tightened the halyards, and dried out the small boxes that held the flags, and re-rolled the bunting. The skipper sat on his chair looking down to the bows, smoking his pipe; things were getting back to normal. The galley re-opened, and the chef was once again the butt of many jokes.

Going ashore in Fremantle we were stopped along the street by people who had recently arrived. They had taken advantage of a joint government initiative between the British and Australian governments allowing British subjects to travel and settle in Australia after paying £10.00 for their passage. Thousands of people left the U.K. and being as Fremantle and Perth were the nearest ports the majority of them settled here.

Many of these people were homesick, and out of work. They longed for news of home. They asked you where you came from, wanted to know what was going on "in the old country" and would we write to them.

However, the reception we received in the bars was none too cordial from the Aussie sailors. Their navy at the time was largely made up from old American wartime 'Tin Cans'. They referred to us as 'Kippers', implying we had no backbone. The locals named the new arrivals from the old country as Ten Pound Poms. We found their attitude to be pro-American, rather than British. Arriving in Perth, it reminded me of a small British town of perhaps thirty years ago, but once again the Aussie sailor's attitude was very much like we had come across in Fremantle.

After a few days there we sailed south to the small town of Albany. Two whaling ships were tied up alongside, which was the main reason for the town's existence. It was a small community, with few houses, a church, and two pubs. It was in one of those pubs I saw the one and only kangaroo I was to see in Australia. It was chained up at the back of one of the pubs we visited. It was a sad-looking creature, no doubt for being chained up, and its coat had several bare patches, giving it an appearance of a moth-eaten blanket.

Sailing from Albany we steamed along the bottom of the country and up the east coast to Brisbane. The men-only pubs there were jam-packed, but at 6pm, when the doors closed and everyone found themselves outside on the pavements, we found ourselves with nothing to do.

Strangely enough we never heard the expression Ten Pound Poms in this part of the country, but the Aussie sailors still insisted on calling you Kipper. Whilst standing there on the pavement outside the pub, I noticed a red glow far in the distance. I asked a passerby what it was.

"It's a bush fire, it's been going for a few days now, nothing to worry about," he said. We sailed from Brisbane, stopping at Manus Island for a quick re-fuelling stop, and then once again back to Hong Kong.

This was our last visit and I went to the Lucky Seven bar to see Ah Kum. She wasn't there. Bitterly disappointed, I boarded the tramcar and went to the shack area in Wanchia to look for her. Entering, in what I knew was her place, I found her lying asleep on her cot. I did not see mumma san and the curtain was not hanging up. I sat on the empty cot and gently shook Ah Kum awake. She opened her tear-stained eyes, and in the first instance she did not recognise me. Then she sat up, and without saying a word she came over and put her arms around me and burst into tears.

Mumma san had died a day after the ship had left. Bereft, she turned to the other girls in the bar. They had mumma san cremated, and now Ah Kum had no options left.

I shared her grief, and lay down beside her. We were both crying, and after a restless night we awoke in the early morning. I had to tell her I was not coming back to Hong Kong as the ship would be leaving for Singapore later that day, and the crew would be flown home from there.

I considered not going back to the ship, but realised this was not an option that was open to me. Saddened by the whole situation, I plucked up enough courage to tell precious Goldie that I would not be coming back.

I did tell her, and when dressed to leave, she came to me and said, "Here is a present from mumma san." She handed me two embroidered patches of Chinese dragons. I thanked her and held her in my arms for the last time.

I made my way through the shacks, and caught a rickshaw back to the ship. Once on board I sewed the two dragons on the inside of the cuffs of my blue suit.

EIGHTEEN

UNDER THE MUSHROOM

H.M.S. *Cossack* slipped out of Hong Kong Harbour under the cover of darkness one October night in 1957. There were no waving well-wishers or pretty women from the girlie bars, just dockyard mateys to let go the berthing lines. The ship had been darkened, the only lights switched on being the masthead, port and starboard navigation lights. We had provisioned ship and embarked a handful of civilians who brought with them several large wooden crates.

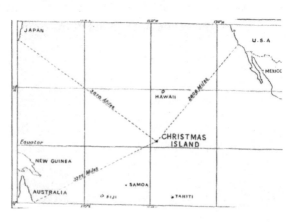

The crew were a mixture of veterans and youngsters. Most of the experienced sailors had served at sea in the Atlantic, or Russian convoys of the Second World War, and later in Korea. Amongst the youngsters (mainly teenagers) some had been to sea before, but there were others who had not. I had done some sea time before joining *Cossack* and felt like an old salt, but in truth, the fact being, I was still wet behind the ears. I was still classed as 'under age' so consequently did not draw a tot of rum.

The ship's company had blended well together during the work up period, and had drilled, and then drilled again, until the captain was satisfied we could run our ship in a seaman-like manner worthy of the best traditions of the Navy. The captain was well liked and respected; all this made for a happy ship.

After several days at sea we approached the sandy atoll of Pulo Tioman in the Pacific at a slow, steady pace, almost a majestic pace, and dropped anchor facing the white pristine beach. Beyond the beach stood palm trees encircling the island. Later that afternoon after the daily ration of rum had been consumed, the crew would wade ashore to enjoy a barbeque. The ship's butcher carried a frozen pig's carcass ashore on his shoulder, followed by a train of willing helpers holding all the supplies necessary for a glorious feast, and a riotous sing-song where traditional naval songs, some more risqué than others, were lustily belted out. It was not only the lower deck who had their songs, as the wardroom officers also had their repertoire. Some of their songs were parodies of Gilbert and Sullivan tunes with hilarious stanzas. We sang songs that had been in the Navy since our ancestors' days. For us young ones, this is how we learnt the words so we could join in the sing-songs at the various fleet canteens.

Both watches had been ashore so on the third day we upped the anchor and steamed off into the Pacific once more.

After several days at sea the captain mustered the ship's company on the upper deck and informed us of our mission. We were to assist the scientific people in monitoring and measuring the fallout from the hydrogen bomb which would be detonated some miles off Christmas Islands. He went on to explain that the fallout would be minimal, but this may be difficult to achieve considering this detonation would be 1000 times more powerful than the atom bombs dropped over Hiroshima and Nagasaki twelve years previously.

Christmas Island was unknown territory to the ship's company of *Cossack* but was well known to the 4,500 British servicemen that were stationed there in 1957. There were members from all three services, but the vast majority were Army personnel. Apart from servicemen on the island there were numerous feral dogs and cats. Some of these dogs and cats were adopted by the servicemen, but as there were no veterinary services on the island the numbers greatly increased in a very short space of time.

This medium-sized island of about 120 square miles enjoys a warm climate and a pristine environment. The island is surrounded by shallow waters and the largest coral atoll in the world. Large areas of the island are covered in monsoonal forest, where millions of large red crabs live, but migrate to the coast every year between October and December.

In 1942 the Japanese had captured the island and evacuated over half of the population to Surabayan prison camps which left only 500 Chinese and Malays to survive as best as they could. These people had come to Christmas Island when phosphate had been discovered and began to be mined. Shortly after the war the Allies reoccupied the island.

We started our patrol to keep all shipping out of the area. We were to spend the next sixty-three days continually at sea. It was a long and arduous time.

Constantly refuelling, and replenishing at sea, whilst the 'Boffins' unpacked their wooden crates and installed their instruments in various locations on the upper deck.

All ships intercepted complied with our request to alter course and leave, until two days before the test a

Japanese fishing vessel carrying anti-nuclear protesters adamantly refused to leave. The captain ordered the guns crew to man the guns and had them trained, almost at point blank range upon the fishing vessel. The skipper of the vessel then turned around his ship and disappeared over the horizon.

November 8th 1957, 'Operation Grapple'

It was a gorgeous bright sunny day without a whisper of a cloud in sight. Not a breath of wind was present and the sea was so flat it resembled a shimmering plate of glass. We had seldom seen the sea like this before. The silence on deck was broken when over the ship's tannoy we could clearly hear the pilot's voice: "Approaching target area." Fire hoses fixed vertically to the ship's superstructure sprang to life, spraying fountains of water in every direction. We were dressed in No.8s working rig, anti-flash hood and gloves which we always wore when firing the guns. We also wore anti-glare goggles specifically for this occasion.

The R.A.F Valiant bomber carrying the 15-feet-long cylindrical 5-ton H-bomb, after reaching its maximum flying height of 45,000 feet, had now reached the target area, the *Cossack* being three miles away.

The Boffins were hunched over their instruments anxiously twisting dials and knobs with nervous hands.

Over the tannoy we heard, "Bomb gone."

We waited, in the eerie silence, tensed with nervous anticipation whilst the bomb plunged downward to the prescribed height for detonation. *Cossack* maintained course and speed.

Then came the flash, of such brilliance it outshone the sun, and the sky seemed not to exist. In quick order a blast of intense heat that almost sucked the air out of our lungs.

At this very moment back on Christmas Island a young soldier stood facing the blast, but stood behind a palm tree with his arms clasped around it. The tree was uprooted and John landed 20 feet away with the palm tree on top of him.

We clung to the storm rail, the ship's plates vibrating underfoot. Then came wave after wave of rolling thunder increasing in volume and intensity with each passing second. It was as if a supernatural thunderstorm had gone out of control.

Even in the vast expanse of the Pacific Ocean this barrage of sound would take several minutes to dissipate.

Cossack moved slowly but resolutely forward.

The sea had been sucked upwards and vaporised into super-heated steam. Ahead of the ship we could see a huge column that would form the stalk of the mushroom.

We craned our neck upwards and saw a raging inferno, angry flames shooting upward and outwards raging through black billowing smoke. Rumbling claps of thunder enveloped the ship. The sky had gone dark except for the flames shooting towards the heavens. It was as if hell was hanging suspended 5000 feet in the air.

It was a staggering, terrifying spectacle almost beyond human comprehension.

Cossack maintained course and speed and slowly moved from under the mushroom.

Looking astern we saw a huge column of white vapour, several thousand feet high. Reaching its zenith it began spilling over, forming a gigantic white dome atop the stalk of the mushroom.

Unknown at the time, the 1.8 megaton explosion was 80 per cent larger than anticipated, and detonated much closer to sea level than planned.

As the ship moved steadily away the mushroom gradually diminished in size, and the noise abated. I remember looking up to the bridge and the flag deck just below and saw crew members and nuclear experts clapping and cheering.

The captain ordered the crew members who had been on the upper deck to go through the showers.

We formed a naked chain, and as we passed through the showers we were greeted by a 'Boffin' who waved a Geiger counter wand over us and announced, "Clear."

We continued to steam out of the test area and headed across the South China Sea turning to starboard up the Straits of Malacca to be in a position off the coast of Kuala Lumpur on the western side of Malaysia to assist the Army in flushing out communist terrorists by bombarding their jungle hideouts.

A nuclear explosion of this magnitude vaulted Britain into superpower status and allowed them to sit at the head table with the other two superpowers, the United States of America, and Russia. It changed the course of history, and H.M.S. *Cossack* was part of that.

NINETEEN

THE LAST
COMMISSION

The *Cossack* was to do one more commission in the Far East before coming home. The new crew had picked her up in Mombasa, in June 1958, and sailed for Trincomalee. However, whilst she was at sea proceeding to Trincomalee, she received a signal telling her that once she had refuelled and re-ammunitioned, but not stored, she would have to go to the Middle East. She increased speed, to 23 knots, and arriving outside the harbour found that the ship had not been given clearance to enter harbour and was refused permission to come alongside. The Ceylonese Government had little alternative in their action, for the Middle East situation as it was, we could not guarantee that we were going there on an operational basis.

The *Cossack* now slowly steamed around outside the harbour, until it was decided to anchor to conserve fuel. After a day and a half, the Royal Fleet Auxiliary ship *Arndale* was allowed outside the harbour to refuel and re-store the *Cossack* although there was little stores to be had. As one member of the crew recalls, breakfast usually consisted of a cup of tea, and a Woodbine cigarette.

The captain had now received instructions to take the ship to Bahrain. The ship's company must have been taken by surprise, as they were fully committed to serve on the China Station, and indeed many had volunteered to do this. It is extremely doubtful that any member of the present ship's company would have volunteered for the Middle East. On the other hand they also knew that you went where the Navy sent you, and that was not where you may have wanted to go.

The passage from Trincomalee to Bahrein was made in very bad weather, and one night in the middle watch a life raft and a survival pack was washed overboard. Because of the mountainous seas there were at the time, they were unable to retrieve it. The ship arrived in Bahrain on the 27th July and tied up alongside the Sitra jetty. They were to remain there for several weeks, and the only distraction being the air condition canteen at the small naval base of H.M.S. *Jufair* some eighteen miles inland. But as recorded in their commission book the trek to the canteen was not made too frequently as they would have liked. The canteen had no glass windows, just holes in the walls and the air conditioning unit was fighting a losing battle against all the openings.

Life on board below decks became miserable. Additional fans were bought to ease the unbearable heat. The chefs in the galley were working under more extreme heat and the quality of the food provided to the crew became less than desirable.

But thankfully H.M.S. *Cavalier* arrived on station, and the *Cossack* was to leave Bahrain and go to Singapore.

As was the case in the previous commission, the crew were now transferred to H.M.S. *Terror* whilst the ship underwent a refit.

The ship now completely changed. Anything that could be moved was moved, and that included stores, doors, and hatches, and the three gun mountings! Air hoses and electrical cables from the dockside were connected up and swarms of dockyard workers invaded the ship. This was the scene for the next few weeks. The incessant noise and smoke from the air hammers chipping away paint and rust, and the flames of the welders. Looking from the dockside it appeared as total and utter confusion. Phase one of the refit now shifted to phase two, where she was moved into the dry dock.

The crew's routine had been changed to tropical routine which meant they finished work at twelve noon, and then could go back to *Terror* where they could swim in the pool, cool off and relax. There were a number of Malay and Chinese shops on the base where matelots could buy his 'Rabbits'. One of these was the small tins of 'Tiger Balm' which, if you believed the Chinese, could cure almost all the ills known to mankind, including hangovers and sexually transmitted diseases, and make you fit for double duty. In the evenings, the canteen served ice-cold, duty-free Tiger beer, which made it 50% cheaper than anywhere outside the base.

Christmas was spent in Singapore. The mess decks were decorated and although the captain's wife was not available to do the rounds, the First Lt.'s wife who

156

happened to be Australian, was met in each mess with a rendition of 'Waltzing Maltilda'.

Shortly after Christmas the *Cossack* went to sea for more exercises with the Royal Australian Navy and units from The New Zealand Navy.

Back in Hong Kong after being at sea for a while the *Cossack* sailed towards North Borneo for exercise 'Saddle Up' which was carried out by American and British troops using American landing craft, with *Cossack* in company with American and Australian ships providing covering fire.

It was whilst at Kudat (North Borneo) that the *Cossack* lost one of its ship's company, who unfortunately fell overboard from a local craft whilst coming back from shore, and was drowned. His body was recovered two days later, and then the ship proceeded to sea where he was buried with full naval honours.

The *Cossack* was soon to leave for a trip to New Zealand, and for most of the passage she escorted the Royal Yacht who had the young Duke of Edinburgh aboard for his Australian tour.

The *Cossack* arrived in Auckland and was greeted by the Maoris singing them into harbour. They were to visit Rotura and Nelson before leaving for Hobart, Tasmania. They went on to visit Adelaide and Fremantle, then onto the Philippines where they anchored in Manila. Stepping ashore there they were followed by young boys, perhaps ten to twelve years of age carrying boxes of Havana cigars, and bottles of cheap Jamaican rum all for a fraction of the price that one would pay elsewhere.

As with any commission it was drawing to a close, but the crew would have to bring the ship back to the U.K. On the 6th November 1959 they sailed for the last time from Singapore.

They were to stop at Colombo, Aden, then travel northbound through the Suez Canal to Malta, and finally Gibraltar.

On the final leg of its homeward passage, entering the Bay of Biscay they hit a force nine gale. Stoker mechanic Rees recalls spending twenty-nine continuous hours in the engine room. No one was allowed to leave their station, and no one was allowed on the upper deck apart from the bridge personnel.

The motor boat that was mainly used to take liberty men ashore when anchored out was torn from its davits and washed into the sea. The sea boat on its davits immediately behind the motor boat was crushed, and only one side of it remained on the davit. The other side plus all the oars had joined the motor boat in the tremendous waves that were battering the ship. Paint was stripped from the ships' side, and what paint remained hung in strips flapping in the screeching winds.

However, on December 8th 1959, flying their paying-off pennant from the mainmast, they entered Devonport Harbour.

The admiral of the port sent them a message on their way in. It said simply: That's how a destroyer should look like.

During the fourteen years that *Cossack* had spent on the Far East Station she had steamed 440,000 nautical miles.

A proud end for a proud ship, for all who had served on her.

It was a relatively straightforward passage home until the ship ran into a force eight gale in the Bay of Biscay. The ship became moribund and leading stoker Rees recalls spending twenty-nine continuous hours stuck down the engine room.

The motor boat was torn from the davits and washed overboard. The 27-foot-long sea boat was crushed to pieces on the davits. One half left hanging from the davits, the other half floating somewhere in the Bay of Biscay with the motor boat. Paint on the ship's side hung down in strips.

On entering Devonport Harbour with her commissioning pennant flying from the mainmast for the last time, the admiral in the port sent a signal to the ship: That's how a destroyer should look like.

During the fourteen years that *Cossack* had spent on the Far East Station she had steamed an incredible 440,000 nautical miles.

A proud end, for a proud ship, for all who had served on her.

TWENTY

TIGER, TIGER

I joined H.M.S. *Tiger* in late November 1959, the month she left Portsmouth to start an eighteen-month commission in the Mediterranean. There was a large crowd at South Railway Jetty, of relatives, wives, friends, and sweethearts to see us off. The gangway had been raised, and the Royal Marine band played our signature tune of 'Hold that tiger' as we slipped away from the jetty and headed for the Solent. We lined the decks, and from every vantage point in the harbour and

H.M.S Tiger leaving harbour

along Southsea Common and the beach, people waved us farewell.

H.M.S. *Tiger* did not start life in a positive way from anyone's perspective. Her hull had been laid up dormant on the Clyde for many years whilst the Navy pondered over what to do with her. Eventually in July 1955 she was towed to the fitting-out berth in Wallsend. It would take a further two years and several thousand Tyneside workers to make her into anything resembling a warship.

In 1960 *Tiger* was skippered by Captain Washbourne D.S.O., O.B.E., R.N. He hailed from New Zealand and had joined the Navy in 1927. Pre war he had served on the mighty battleship *Warspite*. In World War Two, he had seen action in the Battle of the River Plate, on H.M.S. *Achilles* as the gunnery officer. Whilst still aboard the *Achilles* in 1941, the ship was ordered back to the New Zealand Navy.

H.M.S. *Tiger* was a magnificent ship in many regards, and the Navy was justifiably proud of her. The Navy wanted to show her off, and as such we were to visit most of the major ports in the Mediterranean.

Guided missiles were in their infancy at this time and not reliable enough to be fitted to the *Tiger*, but her armaments were considered the next best thing. Mounted with two twin 6-inch turrets, one forward 'A' mounting, and one aft 'Y' being manned by the Royal Marines. The rate of fire at twenty rounds a minute was phenomenal. These guns could be used for both shore bombardment and anti-aircraft fire. This was unheard of for a gun of this size. Weighing in at 162 tons and stretching down nine decks to the ammunition magazines it was a marvel of engineering technology, and hydraulic power. It was naval gunnery at its peak. It was only surpassed with the introduction of the guided missile.

To complement the 6-inch weapons system, three rapid fire 3-inch guns were fitted. One, directly behind 'A' turret and one deck above. The other two were located amidships, one on the port side and one on the starboard side. These turrets had an incredible rate of fire of 120 rounds per minute.

Boy Seaman Card, who had served on board the *Comus* and *Cossack* in the Far East with us, had been drafted to *Tiger*'s sister ship, the *Blake*. He was part of the 3-inch gun crew aboard her and noticed that once the gun commenced firing, the excessive vibration inside the turret, would not allow the rounds that came up from the magazine into the turret to sit properly on the revolving loading tray. They would wobble from side to side, and in some cases fall over. This would bring the shoot to a halt whilst the shell was uprighted. It was a serious flaw in an otherwise superb gun.

Roger made a detailed technical drawing of a metal shaped clip that would correct this problem. His drawing was submitted to the Ordinance Dept. at the Admiralty and accepted. The new clips were subsequently fitted to all three ships of the class: Lion, Tiger, and Blake. The Admiralty paid Roger a token amount for his invention, and no doubt Roger had a few runs ashore with his mates on the proceeds.

Having just completed a Quarters Armourer second-class course at the naval gunnery school at Whale Island prior to joining the *Tiger*, my job on board was to be trainer in 'A' turret. This meant I had to sit inside 'A' turret perched on a seat that allowed one to look out the shatterproof glass window. I only came into play if there was a breakdown of some description, and the turret had to be trained (moved) by hydraulics. Under normal firing circumstances I was merely a spectator. However, things were seldom normal during live shooting exercises.

On one such live shoot, after several rounds had been fired, the turret began to fill with smoke. It got so bad the shoot was cancelled and we exited the turret choking and spluttering with smoke-filled lungs. The ventilation exhaust fan had broken down.

The expended three-foot-long brass cordite cylinders were ejected out of the front of the mounting during a shoot, and would roll around the deck. Too hot to pick up we pushed them overboard with our feet.

My working day consisted mainly of mopping up the oil from inside the turret at the bottom of the gun well, and handing tools to the ordinance artificers who were constantly stripping down parts of the breech mechanisms and loading trays.

The *Tiger* now sailed for the port of Gdynia. We were the first British warship to visit Poland since World War Two. As we came into the harbour the Royal Marine band played 'Hearts of oak'. We lined every part of the superstructure. The ship's company, dressed in their best suits, displaying what medals they had, stood to attention as we came alongside. On the pier stood local politicians and dignitaries in their refinery. The Polish Navy band was playing, and every square foot of the jetty was crammed with hundreds, perhaps thousands, of ship workers and local people. They waved, they cheered, they raised their hats. It was a public demonstration of warmth, appreciation, and affection, the likes of which we had never seen before.

As the gangway was lowered onto the pier, people swarmed onto the ship. Within minutes people were all over the ship. They were wandering around all over the ship on every deck and piece of superstructure. Whereever there was a door open they would enter. They were in the wardroom, and on the mess decks. We had to get them off the ship, which did not prove easy. Many were reluctant to leave. Exactly why they wanted to stay was beyond us. It was simply chaotic, but eventually, with as much persuasion and diplomacy as we could muster we got them to leave the ship.

The welcome did not end there. The ship's company were invited for an evening of entertainment at the local theatre put on by sailors of the Polish Navy. We watched conjurers, acrobats, and magicians. Listened to pop singers, and opera stars sing arias from well known works. It was professional from start to finish. It was a show that could have graced any West End London Theatre.

Going ashore the following day we were stopped along the streets. They shook our hands and literally dragged us into the dingy, smoky bars where vodka schnapps were lined up on the bar to help ourselves. There was no money exchanged, but the supply of schnapps was endless. With our newfound Polish friends we drank as if there was no tomorrow. We knew where we started, but seldom knew where we finished. Getting back on board, without falling foul of the law, and without falling down was a quite a feat in itself. Then there was the added complication of slinging your hammock and getting into it. But being young and invincible this was achieved.

The ship was opened to visitors every day, and the sentries on the gangways had a difficult task of controlling the number of visitors.

All good things must come to an end, and after a few hectic but happy days it was time for us to leave. Once again the pier was jammed to capacity with well-wishers as we bade farewell to the waving people. As we cleared the port, the order came over the ship's tannoy system to search the ship for stowaways. Happily there were none, which considering the circumstances was quite remarkable.

The *Tiger* now sailed to Stockholm and entering Lake Malaren we were escorted by patrol boats of the Swedish Navy. Invited to the Golden Hall, the venue where the Nobel Prize awards are given, the crew of the *Tiger* experienced a banquet done with so much style and sumptuousness it hardly seemed real to us coming from a crowded mess deck, living cheek by jowl in a steel box.

Inside the Golden Hall, gold and blue mosaic tiles decorated the walls. The tables had been arranged in a huge 'U' shape and between each member of the crew sat a Swedish interpreter to answer any questions we may have. Behind each ornate chair where we sat, stood a uniformed waiter. On the tables stood silver candle holders. Placed between were sprays of blue and yellow flowers. At each place setting were four postcards of the city and above each place setting were three cigarettes (two Swedish, one English), a box of Swedish matches, and a crystal ashtray. A speech of welcome was given by the Mayor, and then the captain said a few words of thanks to the Mayor, the city officials, and the Swedish people. It was a sumptuous feast, and an unforgettable occasion, thoroughly enjoyed by all. They had pulled out all the stops for us, and as always we could not thank them enough.

Tiger now sailed down the River Scheldt, which is linked to the Westerschelde, and tied up alongside in Antwerp, one of the largest ports in the world. This was the Dutch (Flemish) speaking part of Belgium, and we found the language quite baffling. Being such a big seaport, bars were numerous and welcoming. In the bars we found the locals cordial, and friendly, although language did cause minor problems at times.

The diamond trade, in conjunction with the shipping, were the mainstays of the economy here. In one neighbourhood called the Jerusalem of the North, the Jewish people by and large ran the diamond trade. Eighty-five per cent of the world's rough diamonds could be found here, along with fifty per cent of cut diamonds. There was also a segment of the trade that dealt solely with industrial stones.

Leaving Antwerp, the *Tiger* now sailed down the Kiel Canal, a freshwater canal that cut off 250 nautical miles instead of going around the Jutland Penninsula. Members of the *Kriegsmarine* invited us to their canteen in Kiel, and greeted us in a friendly but somewhat restrained manner, after which we sailed for Malta.

The *Tiger* now entered Grand Harbour with as much

pomp and ceremony as when she had left Portsmouth. The Marine band once again playing our signature tune 'Hold that Tiger'. Also a gun salute was fired to the C in C of the Med. Fleet. Grand Harbour was packed with ships from the Home and Mediterranean fleets. The smaller ships, the destroyers and minesweepers being alongside in Silema Creek.

Malta is an island with no rivers, and no hills higher than eight or nine hundred feet. The original inhabitants had come from Sicily, way before Christian times. In 1800 with the help of the Knights of Malta, the British had expelled the French who had barely ruled for two years.

In 1815, at the Congress of Vienna, the Maltese had asked the British to stay, and the Navy had based its Mediterranean Fleet there ever since. It had a small population of 140,000 at the time, but by 1939 it had doubled, and this was causing overcrowding problems.

At the outbreak of World War Two the Italians and Germans both began bombing raids over Malta which lasted for a period of two-and-a-half years. The government then introduced incentives to encourage emigration, mainly to North Africa.

Two years after the war the Maltese found themselves in desperate straits. There was no work, wages were low, and this time people began emigrating to the new world of Canada, Australia, and the United States. It was not until 1964 that Malta gained its independence and became a republic but still remained in the Commonwealth. In 1979 the last of the British troops left.

It was not long after we arrived in Malta that we found out about the delights of the 'Gut'. The official name was Strada Street. The 'Gut' was a narrow cobbled street that started on a high point and led all the way down to the harbour front. There were bars every few yards on each side of the street. Names such as The Lord Nelson, The Silver Horse, Larry's Bar, Tico Tico, Collini Bar, and the Piccadilly. One was enticed inside in broken English: "English-speaking juke box inside" or "Beautiful girls upstairs".

Once inside you could buy British bottled beers which were expensive, or a bottle of cheap local white wine of Marsavin. This was the preferred tipple, placed on the table with very large glasses. It was not uncommon for us to order a bottle each. Guitars hung on the walls of most of the bars and one of the locals would play the old-time naval songs which we sang along to.

On Sundays, proud parents would promenade their daughters along the top of Strada Street in the hope they could attract a young suitor from the young Maltese lads sitting along the benches lining the streets.

On board the *Tiger* we had a young able seaman named Jonno. I mention him for a couple of reasons as he sticks in my mind. Firstly he was the only sailor I met in my career who was a 'T' (Temperance) rating. He did not drink alcohol, and was paid 3 pence a day in lieu of drawing his tot of rum. He did not do this for the money, but simply because he never drank. Johnno could also speak several languages, and there were occasions when he stood on the bridge between the skipper and the pilot translating the pilot's instructions to the captain to bring the ship into harbour.

One day Johnno asked me if he could come ashore

with me and the rest of the animals I usually went ashore with. I told him we always went down the Gut, but he said that was alright with him. Down the Gut that night drinking Marsavin, Johnno drank soft drinks all night. Arriving back at Customs House jetty, Johnno negotiated the price of the dyso, and accompanied each one of us back on board, making several trips back and forth across the harbour to make sure each one of us all got back on board safely. That was the sort of lad he was.

One day he came to me and asked if I would write a letter for his mate who wanted to write to his girlfriend. The three of us sat on the upper deck whilst we composed the letter. Her name was Brenda and Pincher was very much in love with her, although he did not know exactly how to tell her this.

"Well Pincher what do you want to say to her?" I asked.

"Tell her I want to spend all day in bed with her the first day we get home."

"You can't say that Pincher."

"Well what can I say?" he said in a bemused tone.

It took a long three-way conversation, back and forth in a similar fashion before I finally wrote a letter which I thought his girlfriend would appreciate. It became customary for me to write his letters, and I even wrote to his parents at times. I would tell them what the ship was doing, and where we were going. I told them Pincher was well, and missed them very much. I insisted that Pincher would actually write the letter, whilst we helped him in composing it. He never did show us the letters he received from Brenda, but Johnno and I assumed everything was going well. He showed us the letters from his parents who were very appreciative, thanking Johnno, and myself in encouraging him to write.

The ship was to spend Christmas Day in Malta, and on the 29th Dec 1959 we went to sea for exercises. It was becoming increasingly clear that there were still serious problems with the armament. Pre commissioning she had had problems in the engine room, indicated by volumes of thick black smoke coming out both funnels. It was found to be caused by oily rags left in the oil return column preventing excess oil from draining away, but this had been rectified.

We had not up to this time ever achieved the rate of fire that was expected. There would be either a serious oil leak from the hydraulic system, or an electrical malfunction. Consequently the ship would have to go into the dockyard for emergency repairs.

In January and February of the new year (1960) the problems continued, but leaving these behind we left for a visit to the Italian port of La Spezia, then the south of France to Menton, and Monte Carlo. The ship anchored out in the bay would be floodlit at night, and was an impressive sight from shore. These visits were short and sweet, and our run ashore funds did not go very far in the Cote de Azure resorts.

On to Valencia, where we joined aficionados at the Plaza de Torres. It was indeed a thrilling spectacle in the sun-drenched arenas. El Cordobes was the number one and the highest paid matador at the time, and thousands of people would follow him around the country to see his performances. Families brought picnic baskets and bottles of wine to these contests, which for many was the highlight of their week. The pre-fight parade, with the matadors in their highly decorative and sequined suit of lights, the music, and the enthusiastic crowds created an electric atmosphere. As I have grown older, however, I have lost all enthusiasm, and view bull fighting in a completely different light.

At sea again, exercising with the carriers *Ark Royal*, *Albion*, and the two Daring-class destroyers *Daring* and *Defender*, we ended up back in Malta where *Tiger* once again had to undergo another refit. This would take another couple of months as specialists and 'Tiffies' once again stripped down both the 6-inch and 3-inch guns. Perhaps this time the problems with the guns could be finally settled.

Late May we left for exercises with ships of the French Fleet, and the American carrier USS *Forrestal*. A daytime live shoot saw *Tiger* bring down the red chute of the target. Another chute was flown over, and the *Forrestal* opened up. As each shell exploded in the sky it left a black puff of smoke. Within seconds there was a wall of black smoke in the sky, and it seemed highly unlikely that any aircraft would have survived.

On completion of these exercises we sailed for Venice. As we sailed into harbour an Italian helicopter hovered overhead taking pictures of the ship and the ship's company manning the decks. It was an impressive entrance as always. On a personal level it was my twenty-first birthday, and after having 'sippers' all round at tot time went ashore with my oppos feeling rather proud and slightly worse for wear.

We walked across St. Mark's Square, over the canal bridges into the back streets, before coming across a small, dingy wine shop. Inside, on wooden trestles, were huge barrels of wine. One barrel stood in the centre of the room on a block of wood. The floor was covered in sawdust. The proprietor welcomed us in, and we sat on the floor, as there was no furniture in there at all. My mates told him that it was my twenty-firstbirthday, and for some reason, known only to him, he seemed happier about this than I did, because at that moment I didn't know if we were celebrating Christmas or Easter. We gave the happy man a few lira each and he in turn handed each one of us a glass goblet, and told us to help ourselves from the barrel. He then disappeared behind a tattered curtain and switched a gramophone on. Italian operatic arias wafted gently through the curtains, and inexplicably into the sub-conscious.

Sometime later, and it must have been several hours, as I was in a semi-comatose world, I suddenly became aware of the music. It was if I was sitting in the Opera House. I saw the orchestra, the conductor, and excited people standing up applauding. The hairs on my arms stood up on end, as if applauding as well. A tear of joy rolled down my cheek. I had never heard anything so beautiful in my life. It was absolutely mesmerizing. I rubbed my face in my hands, and pulled myself together. I looked up and the happy man stood there.

"You lika it velly much, yes?" he said.

"Yes," I said.

He disappeared again behind the curtain and when he returned he handed me a folded piece of paper. On the paper he had written: 'La Traviata', Giuseppe Verdi, sung by Victoria De los Angelos.

I thanked him, and put the paper in my pocket.

We left Venice and sailed through the Adriatic to the Italian naval base at Ancona, then to the Greek port of Salonika before returning to Malta. Once again the ordinance specialists came on board to look at the guns. It was an ongoing complex problem to which there did not seem to be a solution. However, other duties bestowed on *Tiger* prevailed, and after visiting ports in the south of France the ship sailed for Naples where the *Tiger* would act as guard ship for the sailing events of the Rome Olympic Games. The *Tiger*'s motor launches would have to rescue any unfortunate sailors that found themselves in the bay should their vessel capsize. These sailors were too experienced for that, so our launch was never used.

On the 11th October 1960 the *Tiger* left Malta for the last time to sail back to the U.K. After brief stops at Cartagena, and Palma Marjorca, we sailed into the Atlantic, and a few days later she anchored in Plymouth Sound.

The following day she entered Devonport Harbour, flying her paying-off pennant to be greeted, as when she originally left Portsmouth, by parents, families, wives and sweethearts. Many would see their newborn siblings for the first time. She had steamed 28,000 nautical miles during her commission, and visited twenty-five different seaports.

The first thing I did when back home I bought the long-playing record of 'La Traviata'. In later years I was fortunate enough to see this on stage in Montreal, Canada.

Tiger would do many more commissions, and go through many different configurations. Her 6-inch turret was removed, and the quarterdeck was used as a helicopter landing area. She undertook many roles in the rest of her active life, but in September 1986 she was towed by a Dutch tug to a breakers yard in Spain.

TWENTY-ONE

WHITE MAN'S GRAVE

Now I lay me down to sleep,
I pray the Lord my soul to keep,
For if I die, as like or not,
Some rotten sod will drink my tot.

If the Far East had been every sailor's dream, the Middle East was his worst nightmare. Daily temperatures in the 100-130 degree range made life a daily misery. Below decks it was often hotter. The upper deck beneath your feet was so hot you couldn't walk on it with bare feet.

H.M.S Messina

The *Messina*'s crew had mustered at Portsmouth and been flown to Bahrain, a small island on the western shores of the Persian Gulf. The British fleet first moved to the Middle East in 1935 and made Bahrain its operational base. A flat and arid desert plain, with untold wealth beneath the surface in the form of oil and natural gas.

It was the first state to discover oil, and build a refinery. It had been ruled by the Khalifa family since 1783, who are members of the Bani Utbah tribe.

In the early sixties there were few tarmac roads in Bahrain and even fewer cars. What cars there were, were old beaten up American convertibles. They had plenty of chrome, and huge tail fins on the back end, but doors were not considered a necessity as most had one, or more doors missing. Petrol was 6 pence an Imperial gallon and with a 40-gallon petrol tank could be driven for some time without the necessity of a refill.

Besides the huge refinery station, manned mainly by Europeans, there was little else to make a run ashore worthwhile. It was an extremely desolate land, made worse by the oppressive heat. After the delights of Hong Kong and Japan, Bahrain was total misery. We went weeks, months on end without seeing any signs of civilisation. When we did venture towards land we saw a scenario devoid of life. Sand dunes as far as the eye could see distorted by the shimmering heat from the surface of the sands. No buildings, no human beings, no natural vegetation, no hills or rivers. It was either open, flat sea, or deserted arid sand dune islands.

Messina, built in 1945, was a flat-bottomed floating wreck of the Amphibious Warfare Squadron stationed at

Bahrain. Other ships in the squadron included H.M.S. *Anzio*, H.M.S. *Striker*, and H.M.S. *Narvik*, although the squadron seldom went to sea together and deployed as a squadron. Messina was a snub-nosed vessel built for coastal waters so speed really was not a consideration. Running down the centre of her, almost the complete length of the ship, was the cavernous tank deck.

The ship's company consisted of 104 experienced sailors. There were no boys, or junior seamen aboard as this was a ship that needed sailors who had seen some sea time, could work with little or no supervision, and knew their way around. It was a ship that could not afford to carry any passengers.

We were a tightknit ship's crew. Everyone became known to each other in a very short time. There was none of the segregation between the different departments usually found on bigger ships.

Supplementing the ship's company were Goanese cooks and stewards for the wardroom. They came from the former Portuguese colony of Goa, which had belonged to Portgual for 450 years, before it was annexed by India in 1961. They spoke Konkaki between themselves, and ate mainly rice and fish curry. There was a mix of religions among them, but the majority were Hindus with a sprinkling of Christians and Muslims, and less than one per cent were Buddhists.

One of my mates aboard at the time was Mac. Mckenzie who was a stoker mechanic. If we thought it was hot on deck, it was nothing compared to what they endured in the boiler and engine rooms. When Mac was on watch I would take his tot of rum down to him.

From the upper deck you lifted the hatch then closed it behind you before opening up the next hatch to enter the engine room. It was an air lock to maintain pressure in the engine room. Stepping onto the metal plates on the engine room floor a blast of heat would hit you that would take your breath away. Mac would be standing there in a pool of his own sweat. I would hand him his tot, and I swear it didn't touch the sides as he gulped down his rum as if there was no tomorrow.

We spent long periods at sea going from one place to the other mainly because of the slow speed of the ship, and the blunt rounded bows meant she had to push her ponderous way forward. We probably had an economical cruising speed of about 8 knots which felt as if you were not going anywhere, anytime soon.

❧

In addition to the ship's company there were a total of 168 soldiers and Royal Marines on board. The Marines manned the seven landing craft that swung from davits on the upper deck. Also secured on the upper deck were several 1500cwt. lorries, Jeeps, tank ammunition, and a petrol bowser to refuel the tanks whilst on the move. A tracked wheeled tank recovery monster vehicle completed the inventory of armour stowed on the upper deck. Coils of rope and chain were piled up between the vehicles. Space was tight and limited, and moving around on the upper deck always required some thought.

Down below she carried fifteen Centurion tanks weighing 50 tons a piece, housed in the hanger-sized tank deck. These tanks were to see action years later in the six-day war, the 1973 and 1978 Yom Kipper conflicts and the 1982 invasion of Lebanon. The Centurions were in later years replaced by the Chieftain. All this lot was crammed into a ship of 3000 tons.

She had only one twin-barrel Bofor gun for self-protection, placed well forward, but just aft, and above the massive bow doors. This rapid-firing anti-aircraft gun could also provide covering fire during the landing of the troops.

The ship was old and tired, and never easy to live on. Very little worked the way it was supposed to. The freshwater condensers often broke down which left the crew with no freshwater at all, and strict water rationing was usually the order of the day. On one occasion the NAAFI store had to be emptied of all soft drinks and beer as it was the only available drinkable liquid on board.

The mess decks which ran down the port side of the ship were narrow and cramped. There were no portholes. A small air conditioning unit placed at one end of the mess deck seldom worked and was constantly under repair. We slept under the tables and on top of then.

The *Messina* was rarely given permission by the local Sheiks to come right into harbour and secure alongside because of the huge amount of explosives we carried which meant it usually anchored off shore. Sleeping on deck was not much better. One night I took my mattress on the upper deck to sleep. I didn't get much sleep although it was nice and cool. When I woke up, I found sand in every orifice of the body. My eyes were scratchy all day, and I had to dig the sand out of my ears, nose, and belly button.

On the outboard starboard side of the ship a huge floating platform was secured. The Rhino, a huge motorised floating platform, was used to carry the tanks onto the beaches.

The seaman's lot was one of hard physical labour. We pulled and heaved massive ramps around the tank deck with ropes and chains. We were known as the Chain Gang. Sweeping the tank deck produced clouds of rust dust which would come down on our sweaty bodies, and matted your hair. The sun had by now bleached my hair and eyebrows snow white. We were constantly in the showers. We never dried ourselves off, but simply went to the upper deck and stood there.

The soldiers belonging to the Tank Corps Regiment were no better off. As part of their kit they carried on their belts an aluminum mug, with folding handles. At tot time, they were entitled to a tot of rum, the same as the marines and ships company. I had acquired one of these mugs and sat on the upper deck when the rum was issued. As the mug could hold two or three tots it was was not unusual for the soldiers to tip their rum into your mug, as many of them did not like rum. They were referred to by the ship's company as 'Pongoes' mainly because when they received the instructions that water rationing was to be strictly observed, they understood this to mean that they could only have one shower a day. Also to be fair, they had been placed in an alien environment, and did not understand the nautical language and terminology. They did not know how a ship operated, and got lost attempting to find their way around the ship. Often they stubbed their toes on protruding ringbolts on the deck, only to repeat the same experience a few minutes later.

They must have found life on board very difficult. As space was so tight there was little room for them to sleep. They could be found sleeping in the back of their lorries, and underneath them. Some slept in the Jeeps, others on top of the ammunition boxes. A lot of these soldiers were national serviceman doing their obligatory two years of service. They were a good bunch of lads and despite the difficulties they faced were fun to be with.

The Royal Marines on board were always very physically fit and businesslike, considered themselves a cut above the soldiers. Many had been to sea before, knew the sailors' lingo, and knew their way around ships. They would ferry the troops ashore onto the beaches when the time came.

Landing the tanks and troops shore sides was a tricky manoeuvre. The Rhino had to be let go, and the marine crew would climb down the scrambling net hung over the ship's side and board the Rhino. The marine coxswain would then drive the Rhino around to the bows of the ship and the bow doors would be opened. The ramp from the *Messina* would be lowered and the tanks driven onto the Rhino which would then take them to the beach.

We spent considerable time in the Gulf of Oman, then down to the Arabian Sea and then west to the Gulf of Aden. Aden was one of only a few places in the Middle East at that time that was not a dry country. But drinking in the local bars at that time in Aden was a hazardous night out as local terrorists were throwing hand grenades into the bars used by British servicemen.

To relieve the tedium of shipboard life at sea an S.O.D.S. Opera was organised. The Sailors Operatic and Drama Society was a long-ago society when the British Navy was the biggest in the world. The show was put on in the for'd end of the tank deck. Mac and I did the B.B.C. news, which was followed by a line of dancing 'girls' consisting of four tattooed matelots, with coloured material tied around their waists, and two half-coconut shells tied with string around their chest. The old gramophone cranked out the can-can music as they pranced up and down the impromptu stage. We had another shipmate who had an opera voice, and a Royal Marine who was a stand-up comic. The soldiers on board thought it was quite hilarious as they had never seen anything like it before.

We were several months into the commission by now. It was late in the forenoon watch after several days at sea whilst steaming in the Indian Ocean that an explosion occurred in the engine room that rocked the ship and brought it to a standstill. The sea was calm and the ship floated moribund.

꧁

Two stokers had been killed by the escape of high-pressure steam. Mercifully, they would not have known anything about it.

At noon hour I approached the dreaded engine room hatch with Mac's tot. I had tipped half of my own tot into his as I figured he would need it. I did not know if he would even be there. I opened the hatch door and climbed down the ladder, closing the hatch above my head. I then unfastened the clips to the engine room. Mac stood on the metal plates in a pool of his own sweat. He was pale and drawn. His hand shook as I handed him his tot. Down in one it went. I don't think it touched the sides. Over his shoulder I could see a grotesque mass of twisted metal pipes, asbestos lagging hanging down in shreds, broken pressure gauges with the glass fronts missing. Hissing steam, unbearable heat in enclosed spaces was the stoker's lot. Long drawn-out hours without breathing any fresh air, not seeing the sea or the open blue sky, not feeling the wind against your face. The same few watch crew every time. You knew their family history, and they knew yours. It was the underlying bond that bound all ships together, the camaraderie of your shipmates.

Mac had survived although he and the rest of us were shaken.

As was naval custom the two stokers' kit was auctioned off, and the ship's company bid and paid over-the-top prices for pieces of kit that they would probably never wear. The proceeds of the sale would be sent to the families of the deceased.

The blast had loosened some bottom plates and the ship was taking on water through cracks in the hull. Temporary repairs were made by pouring cement into the cracks, which kept the ship seaworthy and still afloat.

The ship was now taken under tow and diverted to the nearest port where repairs could be made. Towing is a slow process, and after several more days and nights, we approached the flooded dock in Bombay Dockyard.

Once secured in the dock, arrangements were made to have our two shipmates flown home for burial in England. The loss of shipmates is something that stays with you for the rest of your life, and these two lads were no exception.

Swarms of dockyard workers and traders invaded the ship. Welders began cutting out the damaged bottom plates. Holes were cut into the side of the ship; other steel plates were simply welded on to the ship's side.

Because of the oppressive heat our working day began at 7am and finished at 12 noon. The rest of the time was our own, unless we were on watch at sea. It was a good routine for the ship's company but left many hours of total boredom.

In the dock area where the ship was berthed were row upon row of single-storey warehouses full of grain. Atop these warehouses perched big, black ugly-looking vultures with large yellow curved beaks. Every so often they would swoop down and snatch a large well-fed rat. Rats were everywhere. They provided a plentiful supply of food for the vultures who were the only form of pest control.

We entered the dock and the ship's company were billeted on the second floor of a huge warehouse that had been converted into accommodation. The ground floor housed the state-licensed women prostitutes. They lived under strict hygiene conditions, and were regularly examined by a general practice doctor. They wore identity cards around their necks, and as some of us discovered later, they were spotlessly clean, and shaven under the arms, and pubic area.

These women were considerably better off than their counterparts who worked in the cages on Grant and Forest Road in the town area. The cages had bars on all four sides, and held between ten and fifteen women of all ages. Passersby would stop and choose a girl/woman and then approach a man who stood at the gate which opened the cage. After paying the man, the customer would take the woman to a corrugated shack at the side of the road and spend the allotted time with her. She was then returned to the cage until she was required again. Walking down the street here was a pitiful sight. There was always a crowd of men sauntering around the cages, and the outstretched arms of women trying to grab hold of them as they passed by.

The working girls in the warehouse where we were accommodated would come up and visit us once they had finished work. They brought with them bottles of 'gin' which they would sell to us for a few rupees. This so-called gin resembled and tasted like muddy water. We sat on the floor and played cards with the girls well into the night. For a few rupees more one could spend an intimate time with one of them, in a room further down the corridor, in an immaculately spotless room with a small cot.

In contrast to this 'run ashore' the British Women Indian Society frequently sent invitations on board requesting the company of one or perhaps two sailors for social evenings at their homes. These women and their husbands lived the high life in their air-conditioned homes with rooms as large as a department store. A car driven by a servant would arrive at the gangway to take us to the residence of the people who had invited us to dinner.

We were invariably met at the door by a turbaned manservant and after being introduced to the family were offered the luxury of a bath. In any other society this would have been considered an insult but we gratefully accepted the offer. Shown into the sumptuous bathroom where the servant had already filled the bath with sweet-smelling salts.

⁂

After six weeks in the dock, and all the repairs to the ship had been completed, it was time to leave and once again return to the Arabian Sea. No sooner had we left the dock area when we found our first rat aboard. We soon spotted several more and quickly realised that the ship was infested with them. The Jack Dusty, with a little forethought, had ordered two dozen rat traps and we now fixed them on top of the various pipes and cables throughout the ship.

These metal, spring loaded rat traps had serrated jaws that when sprung could have severed a man's fingers off very easily. In the seamen's mess we had two traps each secured above the mess tables where we ate our meals. It was not uncommon to hear the trap snap shut whilst we were eating or sleeping. It became part of the routine.

However, after a few days and several rats later, one of the traps had become loose and the next rat that entered the jaws of death fell onto the table attached to the trap which was covered with bloody and gory entrails. This always caused great merriment, causing a loud cheer. By this time we had a volunteer rat disposer, a rum rat named Geordie who for a 'Sipper' from everyone would take the trap to the upper deck, dispose of the rat overboard, clean and re-install the trap. Opening the potato locker on the back end of the ship we found the top layer had been eaten by the rats, and several of them scrambling around eating the rest.

❧

Geordie was a beast of a man. Of average build and height, he was covered in tattoos mainly done from his time in the Far East. We had several rum rats on the *Messina*, and to be brutally honest I was one of them, but Geordie beat us all. When he spoke to you, even before tot time, it was difficult to understand what he said. After tot time, conversation with Geordie became almost impossible. You could see and hear that he was indeed talking as his lips were moving, but what you heard could have been Swahili. He never slung his hammock, as that would have been too complicated and time consuming. Instead he rolled out the mattress and laid it on the deck under the mess deck table where it would stay for days on end. Geordie never had an enemy in the world, but how he actually remained functional was one of those things you could ponder over for a long time and never reach a conclusion. He was a great guy, and almost fifty-five years later his character and personality are vividly clear in my mind.

We now lost another one of our crew, when the chief buffer, a veteran from the Second World War, was flown home. He had perhaps the most stressful job on the upper deck and at his age should never have been drafted to this type of ship, or this station.

He was flown home from Bahrain. We were sorry to see him go. A younger but nevertheless experienced chief petty officer was flown out, and reaching Bahrain he joined the ship.

We now left Bombay and headed out into the Gulf, and one of the many deserted islands to be found in this part of the world. The object of the exercise was to land the tanks so they could have a live firing.

There were two different ways this could be achieved. Firstly, and this was the preferred option, was for the *Messina* to run directly up onto the beach. The giant bow doors would be opened, and the equally massive ramp would be lowered directly onto the beach. If this option was not available then it became decidedly more complicated.

The troops would be mustered opposite the davits on the upper deck. The landing craft were then lowered to deck level. After clambering in the landing craft they were then lowered to sea level and disengaged from the falls. As each craft veered away from the ship it would take a position away from the ship and slowly navigate into a circle. The landing craft would continue going around in this circle until the signal was given to proceed inshore. They would then fan out in line abreast so that they hit the beach all at the same time.

However, before this could be done the Rhino had to be released, and with a huge splash fell into the sea. Two Royal Marines and a stoker made their way down the ladder over the ship's side and jumped onto the Rhino. Once on board the stoker would start the engine and the Royal Marine, acting as coxswain, would steer the Rhino around to the front of the ship opposite the bow doors.

It was a tricky manoeuvre to keep the Rhino lined up with the ramp. But once aligned the first tank would roar into life. It was always a tense moment. Any false move could see a 50-ton tank plunge to the seabed. As it rumbled forward and approached the Rhino black smoke plumed upward from its engine. When the front edge of the tank tract touched the Rhino its bow would dip about 2 or 3 feet. Moving forward onto the Rhino it would slowly sink a bit more, but levelled out once the whole tank was aboard. The Rhino then turned and headed for the beach. Also taken ashore was the petrol bowser, and several 40-gallon drums of fuel. This operation would be repeated until all the tanks were ashore. Once on shore the tanks would line up in battle formation. As they rolled forward onto the hot desert sands, curtains of sand fell from the linked tracts of the wheel assemblies. Under orders issued by their commander they moved up into the dunes.

One day they asked if any of the ship's company would like to join the tank crews in a live shoot. I volunteered and found myself sitting in amongst the inner workings of this moving beast.

The captain of the tank asked me if I would like to change positions with him. As he was standing up, with the upper part of his body poking out the top, I said yes.

Drums of fuel had been placed among the dunes, and as the tanks rumbled over the desert they would open fire on the move. The whole tank would recoil and the inside of the turret would quickly fill up with acrid, foul-smelling smoke.

The shells were exploding all around the drums, and then there was a direct hit. The drum exploded into a ball of fire, and black smoke curled up into the air.

This was better than the movies, and visions of Montgomery and his desert rats came to mind. To be on the receiving end was a death sentence.

Perhaps this was a consideration in the decision of the local Sheiks in not granting the *Messina* to berth alongside in harbour.

The time was drawing close now for our ship's company to go home.

Eighteen months on this station was enough for everyone. It had aged some beyond their years, others had taken it in their stride, but whatever the effects, one thing it left us all with was a better appreciation and understanding of what we had left behind at home.

The *Messina* was lucky in the fact it had the right combination of officers and men to make it work, and get through eighteen gruelling months. The naval authorities in the drafting office were either geniuses, or had just got plain lucky in putting together a crew that not only worked well together, but had stayed the course.

TWENTY-TWO

THE LAST HURRAH

First the Nab
Then the Warner,
Fort blockhouse
Then Shithouse Corner.

H.M.S. *Carron* was a stripped down version of a 'C'-class destroyer. She had the same hull and upper works as the *Comus* and *Cossack*, but the heavy armaments had been removed. Where 'B' turrets had once been a chart house had been installed. The torpedo tubes had been taken off, and left an open space amidships. Up on the after end the two triple-barrel Squid mountings and the railings that had been used to move the bombs had been stripped away and been replaced with yet another chart house. The 10-ton director which controlled the original main armament of the three 4.5s had also been taken off the ship. One single Bofor gun each side of the bridge were the only weapons that remained. Whereas a normal 'C'-class destroyer would weigh just over 1700 tons, the *Carron* could not have been more than 1200. At this weight, she had a longer range, and therefore could stay at sea much longer than her sister ships of the same class. The downside to this was that she could be tossed around a lot more even in sea conditions that would not normally bother a 'C' class.

Officially she was part of the Dartmouth Training Squadron, but ran from Portsmouth. Her present role was to provide sea time for the midshipmen coming out of Dartmouth specialising in navigation. These middies would become the future navigation officers of the fleet.

Up the trot at this time in Portsmouth was the 6-inch cruiser, H.M.S. *Belfast*, the flagship of the Reserve Fleet. She was skippered by Commodore Ron Young. He had started his naval career as a boy stoker mechanic in H.M.S. *Sultan*. During the Second World War he had been hit by shrapnel. He was a big man, and at this time of life he was bald. His batman and some time chauffeur was my old mate from the China Station, and now an able seaman, Roger 'Ace' Card. He would lay out all items of the Commodore's uniform each morning, ensuring each piece was in immaculate condition. Another duty every morning was for Roger to iron out the creases in the Commodore's newspaper. The Commodore was very good to Roger, and indeed all his staff. When he found out Roger was to be married he told the chef on board to make Roger's wedding cake. Pity I did not know that Roger was in Portsmouth at that time as we could have had some runs ashore. It was often the case in the Navy, and one could miss an old shipmate, and once you left the ship, you would never meet up again.

I reported on board the *Carron*, and went down aft to see my divisional officer.

He was a warrant officer who had come up through the ranks from the lower deck. He knew the ropes. He had seen and done it all, both in war time and peace time. I had nothing but admiration for these men. It was a pleasure, and I think a privilege to serve with officers and men of this calibre. I was reminded of our old skipper, Commander Wykes-Sneyd, who had started his career as a midshipman, and Taft Raymond a three-badge able seaman from my *Comus/Cossack* days who had served in WWII on the Atlantic run escorting convoys aboard corvettes.

"Well Gaffney we have a lot of midshipman aboard and I expect you, and the rest of the seamen, to set an example. Show these midshipman how the Navy works, and how we run a ship. You will be a forecastle man, and gunners yeoman."

I had inadvertently rolled up one of my cuffs, and spotting the embroidered Chinese dragon patch sewn on the cuff of my serge suit, he said:

"I see you have been out the Far East."

"Yes sir," I replied.

"Well you won't get any jollies like that aboard here," he said.

Too bad, I thought.

When I returned to the mess deck I was shocked to see an old familiar face. There at the table sat Pincher, from the old *Tiger* days in the Mediterranean. I remembered the loving and affectionate letters I would write on his behalf to his girlfriend Brenda.

"How's Brenda?" I asked. He looked at me and laughed.

"Well how is she?" I asked again.

"When we got home, we got married, and we have a baby daughter now. We call her Lilly."

We had an experienced crew with quite a lot of married men, and as such, when we tied up alongside, the married men were first off the gangway to go ashore. In fact it was always the single men of the crew who would tie up the ship and stow the gear away. This was a bone of contention that never went away on this ship. Lord Mountbatten had suggested at the highest level of the Admiralty that the Navy should become a single man's navy. This never did happen, but I could see now why it was suggested.

We went to sea almost every day out to the Solent and around the Isle of Wight. We dropped the anchor more times than I care to remember, and spent our days at sea on the forecastle dressed in oilskins and sea boots. Sometimes a midshipman would be there, more as a spectator than anything else, but no doubt they became familiar with the workings of the forecastle.

One day returning from the Solent, Pincher's wife stood on the jetty. I went down with Pincher to meet her. She told me she had kept all Pincher's letters in a shoebox, and was going to keep them to show to her daughter when she got older.

This almost daily routine of going around the Isle of Wight was broken when the news came through that the ship would be going up the Norwegian Fiords, stopping first at the port of Bergen. What better place to go for navigation training.

Once again we sailed out of Portsmouth, and headed up the North Sea to the east coast of Norway. The midshipman stood on the bridge, for all the world looking like the next Horatio Hornblower with their sextants, and plotting our course on the charts.

We sailed up the pristine waters of the fiords close to the rugged sheer cliffs. It was eerily quiet and calm. The scenery was spectacular as anyone who has been there will testify.

Our first port of call was Bergen, a city that sends a Christmas tree each year to the city of Newcastle. We were invited to swim in the local swimming pool. Arriving at the pool with our bathing costumes and towels we were surprised that the local population always swam in the nude. Removing our trunks we jumped into the water and had a jolly good swim.

Leaving Bergen we sailed back to Portsmouth and tied up at North Corner Jetty. We were soon back into the old routine of going to sea on a daily basis when one day a load of packages was delivered on board. There were strict instructions that they were not to be opened until the next time the ship was at sea. On opening the packages we found the latest lifesaving equipment the Navy had come up with.

Bright red, self-inflating life rafts which we were told volunteers would be required to test. Being keen for new experiences I and four other crew members said we would give it a go. We sailed out into the Solent, and then turned to starboard into the English Channel and then headed for the Atlantic.

The rafts were thrown over the side and we clambered into them. The ship then disappeared over the horizon and left us to our own devices.

We sat in a circle enclosed in the raft. It had a small flap that could be opened and we took turns as lookout for passing ships. Darkness fell, as we bobbed around. The sea was moderate and there was not much wind, but we soon began to feel cold and tired. We did not know where the ship was, but we had a small aerial on the roof of the raft so we assumed the ship knew of our location. Sleep was not possible, but we fell into a semi-comatose state. The ration packs had some sealed packs of dehydrated delights which we scornfully refused to open at first. However, leaning out of the flap we scooped some water up, and using the tablets that changed seawater into drinking water, had a drink. We could feel the ripple of the waves though the bottom of the raft. It now began to rain heavily which flattened the tiny ripples. We were going nowhere fast. The mood aboard the raft became sullen and quiet. We were all cold, wet, and miserable but the futility of moaning about it was never contemplated. Hour upon hour passed in total darkness, and silence.

Going for a call to answer nature meant disturbing everyone but eventually nature did call. On hands and knees I made my way to the flap, knelt on the side of the raft and relieved myself. The other four now followed suit. Ablutions over, the stomach reminded us we were hungry. Out came the hard tack biscuits. This time the entire rations of the raft were now devoured.

We only knew the passage of time when dawn broke and the first light of a new day dawned. It cheered our spirits no end. The wind had now increased and we could feel the raft being blown along now. The sea had stirred and waves began breaking over the raft at times flattening the roof. We closed the flap and waited. We waited some more, how long, it was impossible to tell. The sea would lift us up to the top of the waves, and the wind would blow us down into the trough. Up and down we went. It seemed to be an eternity. Up and down, would it never end? I thought of the war time sailors that had been shipwrecked at sea, clinging to wreckage covered in fuel oil. Comparatively, this was a stroll in the park.

The young midshipman was looking deathly pale, and green about the gills. "Don't you be sick in here," we told him. He crawled to the flap and opened it. He hung his head over the edge of the raft. As he vomited the wind blew the contents back into his face. The next wave washed his face and he withdrew rather rapidly back into the raft and closed the flap. Rather sheepishly, he sat down in his position in the raft. His hair was matted in vomit, but we did not have the heart to tell him.

I was beginning to think we had been suckered into this by the Navy, just to see how much aggravation we could take. Then, out of nowhere we heard the ship's siren. Opening the flap we saw the ship approaching. What a welcome sight she was. She sidled up alongside us. We climbed the ladder and stood on the deck.

The lads gave us a cheer, and in the mess at tot time it was 'sippers' all round. There was much hilarity and mickey taking. I am sure that in the chiefs' and petty officers' mess and the wardroom the same scenario took place.

We continued our routine of going to sea almost on a daily basis, but my time in the Navy was coming to an end. I had let my kit run down to the bare minimum, not replacing worn or torn items. One night after coming in from sea and wanting to go ashore I found I didn't have a decent suit. I asked Slinger Woods, who was the killock of the mess, if I could borrow his suit. Slinger was a leading seamam with a first-class gunnery rate with three good conduct badges. He said this would be alright but I had to wear a Burberry to cover the uniform.

Everything went well until closing time at the Lennox, when walking back through the dockyard gates I remembered I had left Slinger's Burberry there. I knew if I went back there to get it they would not let me in so I never went back there. I walked up the gangway and my divisional officer was there as officer of the watch. He took one look at me and walked over to the other side of the deck and looked across the harbour. It was a lucky break. Any other officer would have had me up in front of the captain lifting my hat as a defaulter. The next morning the D.O. approached me on deck and said, "Gaffney, if you get many more promotions I will be saluting you!" And that was the end of it.

Shortly after this I received my final draft chit into the Royal Naval barracks in Portsmouth to do the discharge routine. I packed my kit and said goodbye to my divisional officer and mess mates.

In an effort to rehabilitate sailors and make the transition to civilian life easier the Navy offered three vocational courses. They were given by civilian instructors and lasted three weeks. Perhaps the Navy considered our attention spans were not sufficiently capable of absorbing any instructional course for a longer period. In three weeks, according to the Navy, and the teacher, we could become one of the following:

1) A carpenter, 2) A welder, or 3) A bricklayer. How this was possible I did not know.

For no particular reason I chose to do the welding course. The next three weeks were spent wielding a welding torch, and banging red-hot metal on a blacksmith's anvil. I had no interest at all in what the instructor was vainly attempting to teach us, and certainly less ambition to ever pick up a welding torch ever again once this exercise in futility was over. I did meet one old ex matelot many years later who had done the same course, and made a very good living at it, which goes to show it was not a waste of time for everyone.

Once the course was over I had about two weeks to go before discharge day. The final days were spent picking litter up around the barracks and returning items of kit. Going into the drafting office one day purely out of curiosity I listened to a conversation between the drafting petty officer and a young lad who was being drafted to the Far East. Judging by the conversation he was not too happy about it.

I followed him out of the drafting office and tapped him on the shoulder. "What's the matter with you?" I asked. "Well I just met this girl, and these bastards are sending me away for eighteen months."

I told him how lucky he was and told him how much I had enjoyed it, and a civilian would have had to pay a lot of money for the same experience what you are getting paid for.

He looked at me with a bemused look on his face, as if to say, "Are you talking to me?" He then told me to "Feck off". I have often wondered since how he got on.

My final day in the Navy came. I walked through the gates of Victory Barracks in Portsmouth for the last time. My Navy time was over. Walking along Queen Street I never felt so alone and alienated as I did at that moment. I was in a complete daze. I had lost the camaraderie of my shipmates which had sustained me through my entire career, and lost a whole way of life in a single moment.

I had two weeks' pay in my pocket, and a railway ticket to Crawley in Sussex where my mother lived. I had no notion of how things worked outside of the Navy. I had lived in a structured environment almost from birth, and been told what to do, and when to do it.

I did not know how, or where to find a job, or what job if any I could do. Certainly anything I had been taught in the Navy was never going to be applicable out in Civvy Street. I did not even know what Income tax was.

I walked into the smoke-filled Lennox pub. As usual the three musketeers sat at the bar, rolling fags made from Pussers tickler. I bought Big Sylvie, Sweaty Betty, and Terrible Tina a pint of scrumpy each and thanked them for the small loans they had given me over the last few months. I left my railway ticket on the top of the bar, telling the barman to give it to anyone who may want it. At closing time in mid-afternoon I went next door to the Portsmouth railway station and bought a ticket to the unknown world of London, and beyond.

TWENTY-THREE

IN TO THE FUTURE

I never did meet my father. After the war he left England and went to live in South Africa. After managing several hotels he eventually bought his own hotel. He also got involved in politics again, and when Rhodesia declared independence he became the Secretary of the Independence League working with Mr. Ian Smith the Prime Minister at the time.

In March 1967 whilst attending a black tie dinner function he choked to death on a chicken bone. In South Africa he was always called 'The Commander' so it was fitting that at his death his ashes would be scattered at sea.

Accordingly on May 1st 1967, the funeral party boarded the S.S. *City of Dundee*, a merchant freighter, and scattered his ashes off the East African coast where he had spent so much time at sea in World War One. He had spent the majority of his life at sea, and it was where he belonged.

After leaving the Navy, I found myself at a loose end, not knowing what to do, or where to go. After spending a few weeks working behind the bar at a pub outside Paddington station, and being thoroughly disillusioned with the whole business, I returned to Crawley, Sussex where my mother lived.

When I arrived there she was just leaving to see Uncle Harry down at Brighton. Harry was an old sea dog, many years retired, and lived in a comfortable house on the cliff tops at Saltdean, near Brighton. After we settled in, and consuming a considerable amount of Harry's cocktail cabinet, Harry turned to me and said.

"Well Pat what are you going to do with yourself now?"

I had been dreading this question as I knew without doubt that somewhere along the line he would ask me. I did not have one iota of how to answer, but thankfully he rescued me from answering, as he followed this up with: "Why don't you go to Canada?"

If Harry had said why don't you go to Timbuktu I think I would have gone there. Fortunately he did say Canada, although I had never been anywhere near this part of the world.

Harry then went to his writing desk and wrote out a cheque, which he handed to me.

"Go to the travel agent and buy yourself a ticket."

In the travel agents shop when I told the guy I wanted a ticket to Canada he laughed.

"It's a mighty big place, which part of Canada do you want to go?"

"What is the nearest place?" I asked.

"Halifax, Nova Scotia," he replied.

Well I didn't want anything to do with a naval port,

as I had heard too many tales from my Navy days about the place.

"What's the next big town to that," I countered.

"Montreal."

"Well O.K. I'll have a ticket to go there."

Consequently three days later I was stepping onto the frozen tarmac of Dorval Airport in Montreal. The snow swirled around, and the bitter wind went right through my raincoat that Uncle Harry had given me. The temperature was -20 below.

Reaching the customs, a man asked me, in French, Have you anything to declare. I did not understand what he had said. Slightly bewildered I said to him, "Is this Montreal, Canada?"

I thought for a moment I had boarded the wrong plane. He looked at me a bit strangely, must have thought I did not have all my oars in the water.

"Oui Monsieur."

When he saw the puzzled look on my face he then switched to English.

If I thought that it was cold at the airport, six months later I found myself in a radar station on the D.E.W. (Direct Early Warning) line, on Resolution Island, where temperatures could drop to - 65 degrees below freezing. Perhaps I should have stayed in the Navy, I thought.

Having spent thirty-one years in Canada, I returned home to settle back in England. I joined the H.M.S. *Cossack* Association and met up with old shipmates from the China Station. Everyone in the Association had served on her at one time or another. Some had been on her predecessor, and were survivors when she had been torpedoed off Cape Spartel.

Others had served in her at the time of the Korean War, and some had been aboard her during her last commission when they brought the ship home via the Suez Canal.

Any young lad, or girl, contemplating a career in the Navy today would do well to seriously consider what the future Navy has in store.

Without doubt it faces a challenging and exciting time. At the time of writing (March 2015) the Navy has two super aircraft carriers under construction. They are the biggest warships ever to be built in this country and are planned to be in commission for the next fifty years. The forward island on the starboard side will be used for navigating the ship, whilst the after island will be for controlling flight deck operations. There are no arresting wires, or catapults. Propulsion will be supplied by two Rolls Royce Marine Trent gas turbine generators, and four Warila diesel generators to drive the twin screws. The nine building blocks are being built at seven different shipyards in the U.K which make up the completed carrier.

H.M.S. *Queen Elizabeth* is already in the water. This 70,000-ton floating airfield will carry forty aircraft, with a short take off and vertical landing configuration that has a ski jump flight deck. It will have a crew embracing all three services of the armed forces. There will be 700 sailors, pilots from the Fleet Air Arm, and Royal Air Force, and 250 soldiers and Royal Marines.

Facilities on board for the crew will include a gym,

cinema, four galleys, four dining areas, dental surgery, and an operating room with eight beds.

The second carrier, the H.M.S. *Prince of Wales*, is not so far along in its construction, but nevertheless is well under way. The *Queen Elizabeth* should be in commission by 2020. Her first captain has been named as Commodore Jerry Kyd, an experienced skipper who was previously in command of the carriers H.M.S. *Ark Royal* and the *Illustrious*.

You will not get a tot of rum on board these ships, or a dhobi bucket or a lump of Pussers hard to wash your clothes. You also will not receive 32-inch bell bottom trousers, and will not be expected to climb the mast.

However, you will be highly trained, disciplined, and form lifelong friendships. You will be doing a job that you can be proud of, and earn the respect of your loved ones, and shipmates. Remember every time you step ashore, whether it is at home, or on foreign shores you will be looked upon as an ambassador of this island nation. You will be expected to uphold 300 years of a unique maritime history.

I wish you all well and bon voyage my friends.